A

"Sigrid Macdonald has done aspiring and published writers alike a big favor by publishing *Be Your Own Editor*. It's a highly readable guide to turning a mass of words into a publishable essay, short story, magazine article or book. Anyone struggling to finish an assignment, article or chapter will find useful tips for overcoming everything from the dreaded writer's block to insipid language."

Alex Binkley, journalist and 35-year member of the Parliamentary Press Gallery in Ottawa

"Sigrid will mesmerize you as she spins her humor, anecdotes and good, old-fashioned, practical examples into a web of enlightenment. The best part about this book is the power it bestows by taking you from where you are right now to where you should be, inspiring and encouraging you all the way."

Sid Allcorn, author of Ordinary Woman, Extraordinary Circumstances

"At last, a book that guides writers, step by step, through the wilds of the editing world AND makes it clear that writing and editing are two entirely separate jobs! Well done!!!"

Pamela McDermid, freelance writer and editor in Mexico

"I spent two years writing my first book and did not notice a spelling error in the first paragraph of my query letter, until it was mailed out to over forty agents and publishers. *Be Your Own Editor* is a valuable resource tool for college students and newcomers to the publishing world. Sigrid Macdonald covers common mistakes and provides creative tips to bring your manuscript to its highest level."

Deborah Merlin, author of Victory over ADHD

"Very useful book, and really drives quickly through a subject that many find a snooze."

Anita Flegg, author, editor and owner of The Sharp Quill

BE YOUR OWN EDITOR IS AVAILABLE AS

AN E-BOOK.

Be Your Own Editor

A Writer's Guide to Perfect Prose

By Sigrid Macdonald

Published by Lulu Enterprises, Inc.

ISBN: 978-0-557-31219-1

DEDICATION

This book is dedicated to all prospective writers, new and old. May the tips in this book help to enhance your writing skills, and may you always be excited by the process as much as the byproduct of your writing.

ACKNOWLEDGMENTS

I'd like to thank my beautiful mother, Muriel, who gave me a lifelong love of literature due to her unquenchable thirst for knowledge, as well as my Uncle Magnus, who would invariably interrupt me while I was entertaining a room full of people, in order to tell me that I had used a word out of context. Then he'd leave the party, return with a five-pound dictionary, and read out loud the definition of the incorrect word that I had so hastily chosen, effectively destroying my desire to finish my story.

Moira Allen, editor of Writing-World.com, provided essential information about writing and editing on her website and in personal correspondence; in addition, she kindly brainstormed with me about the book's title.

Francine Silverman, editor and publisher of the *Book Promotion Newsletter*, has been a tremendous help over the years in terms of marketing advice for my previous books.

Special thanks to Elmore Hammes of POD Voice of Experience for his expert assistance, to Jesse Merlin for his brilliant contributions, and to my dear friend and colleague Cheryl Driskell, who produced the awesome cover.

I would never be an editor today without my trusted *Chicago Manual of Style* guidebook or my worn copy of *Eats, Shoots & Leaves* by Lynne Truss. My recent discovery of

Mignon Fogarty, otherwise known as Grammar Girl, has made the continuing study of English a rare pleasure. She can be found at Grammar Girl: Quick and Dirty Tips.com or on iTunes. And I have great respect for the Standard Deviants DVD Library of Learning by the Cerebellum Corporation, which produces interactive DVDs on numerous academic subjects, including English composition, grammar and punctuation.

Table of Contents

Introduction

Whether you are a first-time author or a seasoned writer, you have heard all the reasons why you should hire a professional editor to assess your magazine article, book proposal or manuscript before submitting it to publishers. But are they true? Of course, there are many advantages to hiring an editor but there are drawbacks as well.

To err is human but to forgive is highly unlikely in the publishing world. We all make mistakes. Unless you're a machine, chances are good that you'll make many errors along the way and you won't always recognize them. Typos are easy to miss and sometimes they're quite embarrassing.

You've just finished a short story or a blog entry. You post it or send it off to a website for publication. You're thrilled until you receive a call from a friend who says she got a good laugh out of the part that said the irritating neighbor in your horror piece was "a paint in the neck." Duh! How did that happen? You read it over at least five times but somehow your brain skipped that part, and your spell-check missed it because the word paint is spelled properly.

A professional editor has the objectivity and clarity of mind that you will lack after spending dozens, if not hundreds, of hours on an article or manuscript. He or she will also know rules of grammar that you may not know because ideally, an editor relies on a style guide, which specifies exactly where to place a comma or how to capitalize a certain term.

But there is a downside to editors. They're expensive. Maybe you're a twenty-year-old student and can't possibly pay $35 an hour, or two to three dollars a page, for someone to peruse your material. Or you're a senior on a pension, on disability, unemployed or simply saving for the future. You don't want to pay for something that you could do yourself, but make sure that if you do edit your work, you have the necessary skills to do it well.

Another disadvantage to hiring editors is that often they change the meaning of your sentence, or worse, your entire manuscript! Nobody knows your content better than you. You want to retain your voice and control over your work.

For example, you've carefully written several pages describing the parents and grandparents of your romantic lead character. Your editor thinks this is a form of digression that interferes with the flow of the story; you think that it's essential background information. What to do? You don't always want to kowtow to an editor.

It seems ridiculous to hire someone for a small job like a short story or a business proposal, or for an ongoing project, such as a blog. And if you're a student, it's your job to know how to write correctly. But if you have one or more typos, misspellings or grammatical errors, a publisher will hit the big delete button halfway through your material. Teachers will get out their red pencils and potential customers will shop elsewhere. You'll look like an amateur.

The same is true for bloggers who want to maintain and expand their following. We all cut some slack to nonprofit bloggers and are more merciful when they commit a grammar crime. Not so of commercial websites. Selling something? You had better spell it right or people will click away in a heartbeat. It's not that literacy per se is valued that much in our society, but rather that illiteracy, or frequent errors, suggests to the reader that you may be sloppy, careless or uneducated. And that's the last thing that you want anyone to think when they visit your site; they should be focusing on your content, products or services, not the quality of your writing. In fact, if your writing is good, no one should notice it at all. It should be a given that your site will be clear and concise, and words will be spelled properly.

If you're a serious writer hoping to have novels, biographies or works of nonfiction accepted by traditional publishing companies, you can't afford to have your brilliant ideas ruined by poor editing.

Even if you want to publish a book yourself, it needs to be well-written. Anyone can pay to self-publish a suspense story or family genealogy. But it won't sell if it's riddled with errors. We're in the age of interactivity; as soon as someone buys your book and reads it, he or she can jump on Amazon and rip that book to pieces with a bad review. You don't want to take that chance.

If you're willing to put in some time, I can teach you how to minimize the chance of having errors in your work. I'll examine the most common mistakes that people make, based on the fifty full-length books that I've edited. Then I'll provide a pop quiz at the end of each grammar chapter, so that you have instant feedback about your current knowledge and will know which areas are easy for you, and which ones need more work.

I'll address basic writing issues. For example, how do you deal with dialogue and charactcrizations? What's the best way to handle background setting or to introduce the backstory? If your book is nonfiction, what should you do about references, and how can you make your work more structured and organized? And what can you do when you have a paralyzing case of writer's block? Let's find out. Join me in a crash course on how to become your own editor.

Don't forget to visit my website[1] and leave a comment. Ask me a grammar question and I'll post the answer.

---

[1]   http://beyourowneditor.blogspot.com

Check me out on MySpace, too.[2] I have podcasts about grammar and creative writing tips. Download them to your iPod, and listen when you're jogging or taking a walk. You can also add me as a friend on Facebook[3] or Twitter.[4] I enjoy feedback and would love to hear from you.

Sigrid Macdonald
February 2010

---

[2]   http://www.myspace.com/beytrowneditor
[3]   http://www.facebook.com/sigridmac
[4]   http://twitter.com/sigridmac

Chapter 1 — Confidence Is the Key

I've been a writer for several decades and an editor for the last five years. You would be amazed at how many times prospective clients contact me and tell me that they are nervous about letting me read their work. They slaved over their manuscripts for months and sometimes years. They poured their heart and soul into their stories, and became authorities on their topics.

Nonetheless, when it comes to revealing their private work to a stranger, they feel as though they're taking off their clothes. Finally allowing someone else to see that novel, short story, essay or nonfiction book that they've worked on steadily in the privacy of their den can result in a feeling of vulnerability. It was their baby and they felt excited writing it; in fact, many people felt literally compelled to put thoughts, fantasies, opinions and a wealth of information down on paper. But then suddenly, they felt shy. What seemed so perfect while they were working on it began to look grossly imperfect when they saw it through the imagined eyes of another.

Step back! This is completely normal. We all feel uncomfortable when we know that other people are judging us or evaluating our work. We may have a sudden flash of insecurity.

Is it really good enough? Will anybody else want to read it? Maybe it's just garbage. Maybe we were fooling ourselves and wasting our time. This is unlikely. It's more probable that by the time you have put in nine, twelve or eighteen months working on your tome, you can no longer see it properly. You may be sick of your work and eager to move on to the next stage. Often this is the time when you would call in a professional editor.

Ah, relief! Someone else can now examine your material, find all the little spelling, grammar, and punctuation errors and perhaps point out any larger problems that you may have missed. But you don't have $900 to hire a good editor and you don't want anyone to tell you to rewrite your material.

The first thing to do if any of these fears pop up after you have completed a best draft of your manuscript is to congratulate yourself. You've already accomplished more than ninety-five percent of the population. How many people do you know who *talk* about writing a book but never get around to doing it? Most of them. But you're different. You wrote your book and you finished it. You should be proud.

The next step is to remind yourself why you wrote the book or article in the first place. What was it that made you excited about your topic and convinced you to spend dozens, if not hundreds, of hours in front of your computer screen? Resurrect that enthusiasm. Tell yourself that your work is as good as anybody else's, and believe beyond all doubt that if you had the tools to write the manuscript, the essay, the business proposal or the article, you will have, or you will soon learn, the tools to edit it yourself. Promise!

Chapter 2 — Help! I'm Stuck.

There isn't a writer alive who hasn't experienced writer's block at some point in time. That's why the opium pipe was invented and why prolific novelists like F. Scott Fitzgerald moved on to whiskey when narcotics were deemed illegal at the turn of the 1900s.

Seriously, it can be exhilarating to sit down and write when you're brimming with ideas and excitement, and it can be hell to face the blank screen when your mind freezes like Windows 98.   What should you do to get the juices flowing again?

Some people suggest taking a break. Get up from your desk, stretch, take a short walk, go down to the kitchen to make a pot of tea. This can be particularly helpful if you've worked for many hours in a row.

Others recommend continuing to write. If you're stuck on a particular scene or in a certain chapter, you may want to skip ahead to something that interests you more. You don't have to write in a linear fashion. There is no law that says that you have to start at the beginning and move ahead as though you were working from kindergarten to the end of grade twelve. It's your project and you can jump ahead.

When I was writing my novel, *D'Amour Road*, I frequently felt stuck in the scenes involving Québec. That's because I wanted to add detail about a bridge going from Ontario to Québec, and to describe a golf course on one of the main arteries in Hull, QB. The reason that I couldn't write that part at the time was that I hadn't been up to Québec in a while. So I just skipped over those parts until I was able to visit Hull. I took my tape recorder with me; now a cell phone will suffice because you can go into the media area of your phone and record from there. And I dictated my impressions about what I saw, from the names of the streets to the color of the trees to the areas that surrounded the golf course. That was immensely helpful and enabled me to go back and write my Québec scenes.

Sometimes we're blocked for no particular reason that we can think of. No problem. Just start writing about something else. Maybe you can compose a blog entry or answer an e-mail. Occasionally, it's useful to go back five or ten pages in your document, and reread the part that you've just finished. Polish it a bit and expand it. Then you'll probably be able to forge ahead to the next chapter.

The most important thing when it comes to writing a book — and this is true for anything else that we write, including college essays, blog articles, business proposals, your CV, short stories, etc. — is to simply get the information down. Write your story. Put it on paper. If there are holes in it, you'll fix them when you go back to revise. Don't be critical of yourself and don't allow doubts to trip you up.

Ironically, the qualities that we need to put our first draft on paper are the opposite of those that we need to edit the material. When we're writing, we want to be infinitely patient with ourselves. Park your perfectionism at the door. Take that Type A personality and turn it into a Type C while you're actively writing because there is no need, and no way, to have everything exactly right the first time around.

When you return to your material to rewrite and revise, then and only then will you get tough on yourself. That's when you can be critical and meticulous because you want to catch every single mistake, if possible. And you want to view the material the way an outsider would. But don't even attempt that in the beginning when you're formulating your work. At that point, make your sole goal to write a first draft.

If you can't think of names for certain characters, call them Jane, John, Jim or Julia. It doesn't matter. You'll change that later on. If you allow yourself to spend ten minutes stressing about the name of a secondary character, you're losing valuable time and creating anxiety about the quality of your writing. After all, if you can't think of a name for your heroine's husband, how good can your best effort be? It may be excellent but it will take quite a bit of refinement along the way.

Whatever is true for fiction is equally true for nonfiction. You're writing your thesis and you want to refer to a particular website or article, but the name escapes you. You could check that reference right away or you could highlight it in yellow and go back to it later on, so as to complete the important part of your essay: the body.

Any chronic concern about how well you're doing will interrupt the flow of your creativity, which will have a snowball effect. Don't fall into the quicksand of spending too much time worrying about the small things while you're composing your project. Look at the larger picture. There will be ample time to return to the micro-details down the road.

Chapter 3 — Substantive Editing: Polishing Fiction

This chapter will deal with novels and short stories. What are the important components of writing a great story? Let's examine character development, dialogue, plot and background setting. I'll also delve into transitional sentences, how to keep your writing clean and crisp, ways to avoid using jargon and clichés, how to write smooth transitional paragraphs and determining the tone of your piece.

Characterization

In your mind, you can picture your characters clearly. You know how each one differs from the next and exactly what you want them to do or say. How will you convey that on the page? By using detail, detail and more detail.

I have edited more than four dozen full-length manuscripts and at least two-thirds of them have been fiction. More often than not, character development is lacking. Consequently, I recommend that people think of their book as a movie; now describe that movie to someone who is blind. The readers of your book do not have ESP. They can't telepathically tap into your head to know what you have in mind for your characters. Spell it out as though you were telling the story to a ten-year-old.

Start with a specific physical description of each character. It doesn't have to be long and it doesn't have to occur when you introduce the character; however, we shouldn't get to the end of the book and discover that your protagonist has a purple birthmark on his face, or is six foot seven and came from the planet Krypton, unless you were trying to surprise us.

Make sure that your description is not generic. Don't describe a potential romantic interest as "tall, dark and lanky." Pretend that you're reciting his attributes to a police officer who's looking for a burglar. Every trait is important, particularly the ones that will make him unique. Brown eyes or brown hair are mundane. A nose ring or a skeletal tattoo is not. Give your characters a goatee, holes in their jeans, stiletto high heels, platinum hair, a vaccination pockmark or a military crew cut. Do anything to make them different.

After you've created a strong visual image of your characters, devise a separate page where you can write down all the qualities each one of them has. This can be a biography of sorts. What kind of music do they like? What's their favorite food? Where were they born and how do they like to spend their spare time? Once you have a bio on each one, add this information into various parts in the book. Don't put it in all at once. Maybe in the beginning of the short story or manuscript your twenty-three-year-old graduate student is listening to "How to Save a Life" by The Fray on her iPod while she is waiting for a bus. Later on, she and her friend are munching on Chinese take-in. You know that she'll like General Tso's chicken and her ideal vacation is skiing in Vail, because you have it in her bio.

How do your characters react emotionally? Are they easily angered or unflappable? Are they sentimental and romantic? Or bitter because they've been burned? Put this in the bio. Maria's parents had an ugly divorce when she was quite young. She has trust issues and tends to be serious. Something has to be hilarious for Maria to laugh out loud and she's not keen on hugging people, especially strangers. Maria is dating online and she's yearning to meet a soul mate. That means that she would be easy prey if you want to introduce her to an unsavory cad, or she could be completely transformed, and become vibrant and lively if she meets a great guy with whom she feels safe.

Expound on the emotional state of your characters. They will have a basic everyday makeup and then they'll react to certain situations. By telling your reader how your characters feel, you're making them three-dimensional and identifiable. If you want us to love or hate your hero, start by telling us how he feels and why.

Then move on to what your characters believe. What are their ethical and political philosophies? What motivates their actions? Give us enough information so that we come to know and care about your fictional creations.

Lastly, there is nothing intriguing about a character who is too perfect. Josa Young, author of *One Apple Tasted*, claims that her hero is "beautiful, certainly (at least to begin with), and funny, but he is deeply flawed. Spoilt and indulged, he has no idea of what women are thinking or feeling and is as hormone-driven and indiscriminate as young men I knew."

Just as there can be no story without some sort of conflict or dilemma, truly fascinating and realistic characters are imperfect. They don't have to be criminal or callous, but do strive to give them some less than admirable traits.

Dialogue

Obviously, a sixteen-year-old is going to speak differently than a forty-six-year-old. A grandmother talks differently from a toddler. Someone from Texas doesn't sound anything like somebody from Ontario. (How *aboot* that?) Demonstrate that in dialogue.

Study the way people speak. When you're out in public, listen to people talking. Yes, I know this won't make you very popular and I hope that you won't be evicted from your local

Starbucks, but grasping idiomatic expressions, dialect, inflection, content and slang will greatly enhance your writing. As I did for my Québec scenes in my novel, record your impressions into your smart phone. Don't repeat other people's conversations verbatim. Just absorb the gist of what they're saying and more importantly, *how* they're saying it.

Plot

Sometimes the plot for your story pops into your head all at once, like a perfect egg omelet, and you know even before you begin to write what you'll say and how your tale will end. At other times, you start out writing with nothing but a vague, nebulous idea. Often by continuing to develop the novel and the people in it, they magically take on lives of their own; *they* will tell you what they want to do or how the book should end.

Some important things to keep in mind about your plot: How plausible is it? How likely is it to happen? Even if you're writing science fiction, there's a way to make it believable by creating solid characters and using as much traditional science as possible. Every step of the way, think about the credibility of your plot line, especially in terms of its resolution.

A crazed killer is terrorizing the neighborhood and suddenly at the end of your book, he confesses. There's a way to make this believable and a way to write it so that we will dismiss it as ludicrous. Make sure that you add all the fine points that make your story real.

Background Setting

Adding background information is much like creating characters. The trick is to be as concrete and specific as possible. Don't describe a blue sky or a green lawn. Make the deep blue sky the color of Marge Simpson's hair and the whipped cream clouds hover perfectly over the dilapidated red brick schoolhouse.

Balance the amount of narrative against the dialogue. Some people like to read books with a lot of dialogue and others prefer narrative. Whichever you choose, make sure that you haven't gone on too long with either one. Four or five pages of dialogue in a row can make a book seem lightweight. Conversely, five or six pages of narration may make a book seem dense or dry. Find a happy medium.

Don't forget to use all the senses. People often remember the visual but they forget the auditory or olfactory. Talk about the yeasty smell of scones baking in the oven. Mention the loud, terrifying crash of thunder and write about the itchy feel of that old wool sweater.

Backstory

Where is the appropriate place to talk about how an adult lost his mother to leukemia at age seven, and was briefly placed in foster care because his father was an alcoholic? Find a spot where something reminds the adult of his mother. Maybe another woman passes by and she's wearing Chanel perfume, instantly triggering memories of his long-lost mom. Perhaps he's sitting at a restaurant and notices that the business tycoon across from him is sipping Heineken, his father's nightly treat.

You can insert the backstory almost anywhere, as long as it has some relation to a current reference.

Transitional Sentences

Your goal is to have one paragraph flow into the next. Everything should be smooth and readers should not be left scratching their heads, wondering what's going on, as sometimes happens on TV or in film.

One way to ensure that occurs is to have each opening sentence in a paragraph relate in some way to the previous paragraph. If you can't do that, you may wish to start a new chapter or to delineate your material by creating an artificial break in your chapter like this:

***

This paragraph has absolutely nothing to do with the material above so I'm going to set it apart from the rest of the chapter. I let my readers know that by using little asterisks. And I have formatted it differently so that all of my text is aligned on the far left-hand side instead of indented.

Overkill

Be careful not to overwrite your sentences. Use words sparsely. Watch for terms that are redundant like, "I'm going out at 9 p.m. in the evening." Nine p.m. says it all. There is no need to add evening. It's like talking about "sweet chocolate." The only time that you need to do that is to distinguish it from dark or semi-sweet chocolate. Otherwise, the qualifier is unnecessary.

Some words simply take up space and elongate your sentences; they don't add value. I had a good friend in college who ended many of his verbal sentences with the words, "as it were." What does that even mean? It's irrelevant and sounds pretentious, although he didn't mean it that way.

The same is true of ten dollar words. You don't have to impress anyone with your extensive vocabulary. If you naturally tend to talk and write in polysyllables, no worries, but don't feel compelled to use the most complicated and the longest words in the dictionary. Of course, if you're writing your doctoral thesis, that's another story.

If your characters swear, that's fine but guard against the overuse of any terms, profane or not. I just finished watching *Gran Torino* by Clint Eastwood and quite enjoyed the movie; however, I cringed at the repeated use of ethnic slurs, not just because they are offensive — which they are but they were used deliberately to make a point — but also because they made the dialogue seem less realistic. How many times in one sentence can one person swear and use racist terminology? Even the worst bigots have their limit. Unlike *The Sopranos* and *Sex in the City*, which both used believable, clever and witty profanity, *Gran Torino* went overboard and forgot the important motto that often "less is more."

Common Jargon

Equally tiresome is the use of popular words like awesome, amazing or excellent. Remember how often you used to see the term LOL in e-mail or on chat lines? Finally, people became sick to death of it and came up with alternatives like "ha ha," "he he" or even LMAO. Instead of using the ☺ icon, some people started writing out the word smiling. They just wanted to be different and not to bore their reader to tears. Be imaginative. Find synonyms for commonplace words.

Eliminate Unnecessary Terms

This relates somewhat to not being wordy, but it goes beyond that by making the goal of each sentence or paragraph to be clear and concise writing. Oftentimes we can omit certain terms. Note the following examples of the same sentence that starts out in a clumsy, overwritten style followed by a much cleaner version.

1. Well, both men were in a state of shock but Jeffrey knew the stakes involved here so he did begin to explain. In his explanation he did try to downplay the circumstances of what he thought was the severity of his son's condition as well.

2. Both men were in a state of shock, but Jeffrey knew the stakes involved, so he began to explain. He downplayed the severity of his son's condition.

1. Meanwhile having heard the commotion in the hall and satisfied herself that everything was okay, Janice went on into the kitchen to try to make some coffee and to begin starting breakfast.

2. Hearing the commotion in the hall and satisfied that everything was okay, Janice went into the kitchen to make coffee and start breakfast.

1. Not only was shoveling the driveway hard on his back, but Eduardo also felt that it was dangerous at his age to be out in the freezing rain in order to clear the driveway, due to the fact that he was afraid of falling on the ice at some point in time.

2. At Eduardo's age, shoveling the driveway was hard on his back, and potentially dangerous due to the ice, freezing rain and risk of falling.

Know What I Mean?

You know what you want to say but sometimes it's hard to express. Try to imagine your reader. Could anything that you've written be ambiguous? Could it be confusing? Don't assume that the reader knows what you are thinking. Step back and fill in certain details or clarify to be as precise as possible.

Here's an example: "That ended her short life in Shadow Lakes." What ended her life there? Did she die or simply move? Or did she stay but she never had a decent quality of life afterwards? Think like a reporter and ask yourself all of the W's: who, where, what and why (and, of course, the non-W, how). Once you're clear about all of those, convey them to the reader: "Marrying Stephen ended her short life in Shadow Lakes because they moved into the city right after their honeymoon."

The Old Maxims

Avoid using clichés in language and characterization. We all know about the prostitute with a heart of gold, or the father who goes berserk when his son is denied medical care and holds the hospital hostage. It's not that you can't write about people who have those experiences; it's done every day of the week. Just make your version special. Instead of saying, "Stop to smell the roses," or focusing in on the need to live "One day at a time," devise a synonym or an entirely different way of expressing a similar sentiment.

For example, your prostitute or sex trade worker (a preferable and gender-neutral term) is well-educated. She hasn't been sexually abused and isn't addicted to drugs. Your character chooses such an occupation because she likes the sense of power and control. She is psychopathic and often ties up her clients, and robs them.

Or the father who is enraged when his diabetic child is refused treatment by a heartless HMO kidnaps the child of the CEO of the HMO.

You get the picture. It's fine to do something that's been done before, as long as you give it a slightly different twist.

Setting the Tone

It's important to ask yourself before you begin, what is the purpose of your book or article? Do you want it to be informative, entertaining or humorous? Is it a drama, a comedy or a documentary?

Identify what you want your reader to feel. Inspired? Outraged? Empowered or informed? Your answer to these questions will enable you to set the tone for your book or article. Obviously, if you want the reader to feel uplifted, you don't want to present a lot of depressing scenarios unless your ending is like that of *The Pursuit of Happyness*: ultimately triumphant.

And you want to avoid mixed messages. My sister, Kristin, has a degenerative retinal condition that rendered her legally blind several years ago. She is a fundraiser for vision research, a motivational speaker and hosts a radio show called *Second Vision* on AIRS-LA.org, the Audio Internet Reading Service of Los Angeles, a reading service for the blind. When she first started her show, Kristin had to reintroduce herself to her listening audience during each new episode and to tell her story. Because she didn't want to bring anyone down and she has a fantastic sense of humor, she would make jokes about losing her eyesight. She talked about how often people thought she was drunk or gay instead of visually-impaired, because she was always holding on to her girlfriends' arms.

There's nothing wrong with being funny but I advised Kristin against this in certain parts of her show. When she described falling down a full flight of stairs headfirst, joking about it diminished the impact on the listener. Her story was serious and frightening, and she needed to let people feel those two uncomfortable emotions temporarily before she moved on. If she hadn't done so, her audience would never have understood how tragic and potentially dangerous her vision loss had become. Once that was established, Kristin could return to being a comedian because that's her style.

So, ask yourself periodically while you're writing what it is that you want your readers to feel, and make sure that your words are consistent with that outcome.

Chapter 4 — Substantive Editing: Polishing Nonfiction

All types of writing have commonalities. Whether you are doing a blog, a short story, an essay, a novel or a nonfiction book, you need a clear introduction, a well-defined body of material and a strong conclusion. You also want your material to be structured and organized, especially in nonfiction.

Introduction

I've been a member of Toastmasters International for several years. Little did I know how much what they taught me about public speaking would affect my writing. Toastmasters emphasized the importance of starting out with a dramatic first line or paragraph. You have to grab the reader's attention immediately, particularly in this era of short attention spans.

Perhaps you can start with a question, a quote or a story. Don't begin with a weak opening, such as an apology, an irrelevant story or joke, or a long, involved and poorly worded sentence or paragraph.[5]

That doesn't mean that you need to be sensational. Far from it. Just be intriguing. Write something in the first

---

[5] *Communication and Leadership Program, a Toastmasters International Program,* "Organize Your Speech," page 18, 1999.

paragraph or the first page that will make your reader want to turn the page.

Aside from being unique and captivating, your introduction should state your main position; you will spend the remainder of the book backing up this statement or point of view.

The Body

The body of your book or article will consist of supporting evidence that backs up your initial claim. This may include quotes, observations, statistics, illustrations or your own ideas.[6]

As Mr. Spock advocated, be logical. The best way to organize your essay or manuscript is to be clear. *The Communication and Leadership Program* guidebook for Toastmasters defines organization as "really nothing more than putting your ideas together in an orderly manner. As a speaker, your business is persuading others to accept your ideas, and success comes only when you carefully organize your approach. You must clearly identify the key point of your subject for the audience and then lead them logically toward that point. Merely talking around the subject in a haphazard manner will leave your listeners confused."[7] In other words, get to the point.

---

[6] *The Standard Deviants Present English Composition*, on VHS, 1997.
[7] *Communication and Leadership Program, 1999.*

Make sure that the topic you've chosen is not too broad. Don't write about the Holocaust in general, because the topic is too vast. Instead, you may want to examine the coping mechanisms of survivors of concentration camps.

Continually remind yourself of your purpose: the reason that you started writing your book, college essay or blog post. This will help to keep you on track.[8]

Toastmasters recommends making your topic "timely and relevant for your audience, a topic on which you can speak with some degree of authority, and one to which you can bring enthusiasm and conviction."[9]

Outline

Devising an outline involves jotting down the main points that will be included in your material and subdividing them under different headings. Later on, you may take something out of Chapter 1, part D, and move it to Chapter 5, part E. No problem. Nothing is set in stone in the beginning.

Each point in the outline will address an idea. As you progress in your chapter, you'll develop the ideas by elaborating on each one.

---

[8]   Ibid.

[9]   Ibid.

Use statistics and figures judiciously. If you're writing a scholarly article, numbers are critical but they can be boring. Often the best newspapers, like *The New York Times,* write a story about the epidemic of HIV/AIDS in Africa and start out by telling us about one individual child. We know that child's name, his village, how many siblings he has and how old he was when his parents died. We care about that one individual boy because we feel as though we know him. It's hard to relate to huge numbers in the hundreds of thousands, or millions, so when you need to use statistics, write something anecdotal if possible.

Stay Focused

As Moira Allen, editor of Writing-World.com, says in her article entitled "Becoming Your Own Editor," don't ramble. Decide on your main point and get right to it. There is no need for lengthy beginnings and irrelevant padding in your paragraphs. If you plan to talk about your irreplaceable dog, "Old Sam," don't start off by discussing the dearth of animal science courses in your first year at college. Make a direct statement about Sam.[10]

Scrutinize your writing carefully to make sure that you haven't strayed off topic. It's so easy to do. One thought leads to

---

[10]   Allen, Moira, Writing-World.com, "Becoming Your Own Editor," [http://www.writing-world.com/basics/editor.shtml], written 2001, website accessed January 24, 2010.

another and to another, and before you know it, instead of making a direct trip from New York City to Miami, you're stopping overnight in South Carolina. Ask yourself when you include information, is this relevant to my introductory position? Does this add to my argument? If the answer is no, as much as it may pain you to do so, omit it.

Enthusiasm

Why should I want to read about child labor practices in the 1600s? Because you tell me that it's something worth knowing about. How do you tell me? By expressing passion for your subject. That doesn't mean that you have to inject your opinion or lecture me. It does mean that you need to bring life to the topic. Demonstrate why I should care by infusing the subject with information that is presented in an interesting and unique style.

Toastmasters advocates speaking from your audience's point of view. The same is true of writing. What motivates your readers? What will they care about? Always picture the readers when you're writing and specifically gear your material toward them.

Using References and Endnotes

Several years ago, I edited a book by a man who was writing about a popular social issue. He started out by citing a study from 1988; I encouraged him to scratch that and substitute it with something more current.

Sometimes, the best research was performed decades ago. In that case, obviously you would use it. You can't ignore Freud or Hegel or Kant simply because you're trying to keep your data up-to-date. But if you're talking about the safety of seat belts or food additives, you're much better off referring to the most recent publications on those topics. And if you don't, your readers will notice.

This is often a problem for people who started writing a book ten years ago, put it away and then went back to it. Their bibliography is out of date. That's an easy problem to remedy and it's worth your while to take the time to make it current.

Citing References

There are several ways to cite references. The important thing is to write all of your citations using the same format. If you put quotation marks around the name of an article twice, then do that throughout. Standard format dictates that footnotes will start with the last name of the author, if known, and move on to the title of the book or article. That's followed by the publisher, city and year of publication.

However, you may not always have access to all that material, particularly if you have found a source online. You can double-check by looking up a particular book on Amazon; they will invariably have the correct info, if the book is still in print.

When you're citing an Internet resource, you don't know when it was published. The website could also disappear in three months or a year, so simply state the date that you accessed it.

Here are some examples of ways to reference books, articles and websites:

Gladwell, Malcolm. *Outliers: The Story of Success*. Little, Brown and Company: New York, 2008.

Gardner, Dan. "Tough Time." *The Ottawa Citizen*, April 28, 2002.

Macdonald, Sigrid. "Book Review: Reclaiming History by Vincent Bugliosi." D'Amour Road, [http://damourroad.blogspot.com/], May 19, 2009.

Conclusion

Just as an introduction describes what you will discuss in your book or article, a conclusion wraps up what you've written. Recap once again and highlight some of the most important things that you mentioned, but don't just summarize everything you've stated in your paper or manuscript. You want to leave your reader with a fresh perspective on the topic. You may write about potential solutions to a problem or another way of viewing the matter entirely.

In your summation, don't apologize or mention anywhere that you are not an expert or an authority, or that this is only your opinion! That kind of disclaimer can completely undermine the reader's faith in everything that you have previously presented. End your book or essay declaratively.

In a good speech, Toastmasters claims that people always remember best what they heard last. The same is true of a book. Make your conclusion tight and powerful. Remember what your original goal was when you started writing your article, business proposal or nonfiction manuscript. Did you want to inform, to lament, or to rally people to take action? Write your conclusion with your mission in mind.

Chapter 5 — Writing Essays:
Are We Having Fun Yet?

Hardly anyone likes writing essays, especially when they will determine half your grade, or if you will be accepted into college or university in the first place. Essays are like a mini version of a nonfiction book, and can take a considerable amount of time. They usually have deadlines, so you want to pace yourself. Let's review the basics of what goes into a good essay, including choosing a topic, doing your homework, evaluating and citing resources, incorporating your own personality and enthusiasm into your work, and staying on track.

Choosing Your Topic

It's easy if you're doing your college application essay, because the question was already chosen for you. In that case, what's important is to *understand* the question; sometimes essay questions are double-barreled, such as "Why would you like to attend the University of Ottawa and what can you contribute to the school?" Note that there are two questions here. One asks why you want to go to that particular school and the other asks what you can contribute. Don't spend ninety percent of your time answering the first question and parenthetically responding to the second half at the end of your essay. Split your answer in half and stick to the point.

If you're already enrolled in school and are taking a second or third year class, you probably have the option of choosing your topic. Delineate. Don't choose anything so large that you can't possibly do a good job. For example, instead of writing about great leaders in history who were affected by physical characteristics beyond their control, just write about Napoleon and the effect that his small stature had on him. Or examine the life of Abraham Lincoln and how he was affected by migraines and depression. Or choose six great leaders, and compare and contrast their personal lives.

How much you need to narrow the topic will depend on the length of the paper. Is it three pages or thirty? Is it your sophomore Sociology midterm or your Master's thesis? The longer your paper is, the larger your scope will be, as well as your ability to add detail.

Research

Read the literature. Find out what's out there but don't spew it back at your professor. Digest and interpret what others have written; don't regurgitate what they've said. And it goes without saying that you don't want to plagiarize; that's like cheating on your partner. It may take a long time for him or her to find out, but when it happens, there will be hell to pay. Even if you aren't caught, it's a feel-bad situation. You'll be much happier with yourself if you write your own paper.

Watch Your Sources

No one is one hundred percent accurate. Wikipedia is the most popular online encyclopedia but it's composed of volunteers. The Encyclopedia Britannica has a paid staff and a peer review process. Wikipedia doesn't; it's an open source dictionary that allows anyone to edit an entry. This is called "collaborative writing."

Wiki is the Hawaiian word for quick. There is a disclaimer in the Wikipedia FAQ that states that the online encyclopedia is a great place to begin your research but it should not be your last stop.[11] It cautions students in particular *never* to use Wikipedia as a sole source; it is limited based on the accuracy of its volunteer contributors, and the ability of its editors to process what the volunteers have written. That's like relying on several clever bloggers instead of *The Washington Post* or the popular Toronto paper, *The Star*; your bloggers could be right but the papers have been in the business of providing news for decades. They have the resources to provide you with the most

---

[11]   "Is Wikipedia Accurate and Reliable?", Wikipedia.com, [http://en.wikipedia.org/wiki/Wikipedia:FAQ/Schools], website accessed December 26, 2009.

up-to-date information, and they have a legal team behind them in case they're sued for defamation or incorrect material.

However, a 2005 study in the journal *Nature* found that Wikipedia was *almost* as reliable as Britannica. The study determined that each article in Britannica had 2.92 mistakes, whereas Wikipedia had 3.8 mistakes.[12] Wow, that says two things: first, both encyclopedias made errors! That means that you must look for multiple sources. Second, Wikipedia is not far behind the major giant, Britannica.

Your best bet is to cite something from Wikipedia and double-check it elsewhere. Make sure that you can find a secondary resource to back it up.

The most reliable Internet resources are run by government agencies, newspapers, foundations and other large organizations. That doesn't mean that blogs are inaccurate but you do want to verify their material. And if you are dying to cite an obscure blogger, make sure to mention where you gleaned those facts.

Don't forget the library. The Internet is quick and painless; you never have to leave the comfort of your chair. But

---

[12] Terdiman, Daniel, "Study: Wikipedia as Accurate as Britannica," [http://news.cnet.com/Study-Wikipedia-as-accurate-as-Britannica/2100-1038_3-5997332.html], website accessed January 26, 2010.

some of the best data may be on the stacks of your school library.
Make sure to include it.

Citing Resources

Writing an essay or term paper is similar to writing a
nonfiction book. Use the same footnote and reference format that
is outlined in Chapter 4 for nonfiction works. Of course, this is a
matter of individual style; some people prefer brackets to indicate
URLs whereas others use parentheses or commas.

Your Point of View

Inject a bit of your personality into your essay. You want
to differentiate yourself from Gina or Jean-Luc who sits next to
you in class. But don't go overboard. A college essay is not a
forum for editorializing. Think of writing a letter to the editor of
your newspaper or an op-ed piece versus being a reporter for a
feature story. If you write about the paucity of services for the
disabled in your town, you may want to say that the sidewalks are
broken down and need repair, many public buildings are
inaccessible because the walkways are slippery in the winter, and
the elevators inside are often broken.

In an editorial or letter to the editor, you can explain the
situation and tell the world that you disapprove. It's fine to add
an emotional element by saying that this is disgraceful. However,

as a reporter, you would simply state the facts. They would come from your own slanted perspective, admittedly, but you wouldn't add words like terrible or unimaginable. Ditto for your essay.

If you strongly believe that your town is inaccessible for people with disabilities and that this is unacceptable, that will shine through in your essay based on the facts you choose to present. As Disraeli said, there are "liars, damn liars and statistics." You can cherry pick your facts to back up your argument, but I wouldn't recommend it. It's better to be fair and balanced.

Let's say that you're writing about the benefits of universal healthcare but you decide not to include any of the disadvantages. That will make for a slanted argument and limit the utility of your paper. You can still argue in favor of universal healthcare while admitting that there are drawbacks, such as long waiting times for certain surgeries or inadequate diagnostic machinery in countries such as the UK and Canada.

Adding Spunk

It's easy to make a college essay boring, particularly if the topic is boring to you. Add passion to your topic. Guard against presenting one statistic after another, which makes for tedious reading. Break your material down, so that after you present someone else's opinion, you pause and offer your own interpretation.

Get to the Point

Think of Twitter and how you have to limit your status update to 140 characters. What does that involve? Compromise. Getting down to bare bones. Essays have word or page limits. Chop and remove anything that doesn't enhance your argument.

Watch for digressions, but don't worry about them while you're writing. When you reread your material, ask yourself on every page and every paragraph, does this relate to my topic? Is it in the right place? Does it flow logically from the last page or paragraph? Is my writing clear and organized?

You may have to move paragraphs around, which is a breeze thanks to the cut-and-paste feature in Microsoft Word. Maybe paragraph three on page nine fits better on page twelve. Do whatever is necessary to make your paper flow smoothly and to present a cogent argument.

Watch Your Language

No, I'm not talking about the hazards of sounding like Eminem or Denis Leary in your Philosophy midterm. You already know that. The language that I want you to be aware of is using polysyllables, which is a vocational hazard for academics.

When I was in grad school, one of my teachers pulled me aside to tell me that, if I continued to write the way that I had been, no one but my colleagues would ever understand me. That made me stand up and listen! Since then, I've been very conscious to make my writing clear and understandable.

Aside from million dollar words, avoid writing long sentences and paragraphs. Paragraphs that ramble endlessly are difficult for professors to read. And don't incorporate any cute little symbols that are meant for text messaging or social networking, such as ROFL or winky faces. That's a big no-no in academic writing.

Acronyms

Many of us automatically use acronyms and abbreviations. We may refer to ACORN or FEMA in our speech. This is fine but in writing we don't want to assume that our readers know what we are talking about; books, articles, blog posts and many other forms of writing are now international. If you use an abbreviation, spell it out first, and then use the acronym. For example, "The Federal Emergency Management Agency, or FEMA, is a government program that prepares for and responds to disasters."

Extra Credit, Anyone?

If you want to really polish the old apple, subscribe to Grammar Girl's quick and dirty tips for writers at http://grammar.quickanddirtytips.com/. You can download them to your iPod via iTunes, or receive a daily e-mail update. You can't go wrong by striving to improve your English composition skills on a regular basis. The effort will be reflected in your grades in no time.

Trick Question

Why did I name this chapter "Writing Essays" instead of "Editing Essays"? Because unlike authors, students are almost always their own editors. Editing and writing aren't all that different from one another; editing is just another name for rewriting, restructuring and revising what you've already written.

Chapter 6 — My First Draft Is Finished. Now What?

Finally, after reviewing your material thoroughly, you have your best first draft. Incredible. You have really written a book, and now it just needs to be polished and perfected. What should you do? Put it in a drawer.

"What? No, that's ridiculous," I can hear you saying, but in fact, the smartest thing that you can do after spending so much time with your material is to take a break from it. Hide it in your file cabinet and don't show it to anyone. Go back three or four weeks later.

Yes, I know it feels as though you've left the baby in the cupboard and he's crying out to you. It's painful. You want to move forward and this seems like stagnation. You want to skip this step because it sounds stupid — maybe it's necessary for some people but not for you.

I strongly advise against that. None of us has a proper perspective on our material when we have been immersed in it, day in and day out, for many months or years. The minute that beloved book goes on the back burner and you become busy with other projects, the cobwebs start to unravel in your mind. You think about other things and miraculously, when you return to the manuscript, it looks different.

This is when certain typos that you missed originally are much more likely to shout at you and wave hello. How could you have missed the lack of an article in the phrase "on my way to museum?" Is it really possible that you spelled the word "cup" as "cusp?" What were you thinking?

Giving yourself time and space away from your article, short story or manuscript will provide you with a fresh start. It is almost as though *you* have become the second pair of eyes that you had hoped an editor would be, because now you can see your material much more objectively.

Not everyone has the luxury to put material away for several weeks; students and business people have strict deadlines. In that case, walk away from your work for as long as you can, even if it's only fifteen minutes or a few hours. You'll be surprised at how different something looks once you leave your workstation and clear your head.

You should now be able to find many, if not all, of the mistakes that you missed initially in terms of spelling, grammar, punctuation and typos. Later on we will look at something much trickier: how to correct problems that you weren't aware of. But for now, let's stick with the easy stuff.

In order to catch those nasty little typos as though they were mosquitoes in a net, there are some tricks that you can use. I always magnify my screen right up to 150 percent. If someone were to look at my computer, they would conclude that I was half blind. When I'm reading for fun, I never do that but when I'm proofreading material for clients, I want to make sure that every typo jumps out at me. One of the simplest ways to do that is to set my view at 125 to 150 percent of the screen.

Another great way to decimate typos is to print out a hard copy of your manuscript and take it somewhere else. If you've been working at your desk, take the printed copy to the library or to Starbucks (bring your earplugs), or buy a large clipboard and take it to the park. It's not important *where* you go, but do go someplace different from where you have been working, and work on a hard copy as opposed to virtual. Bring a red pen and get to work.

It goes without saying that it's much easier to proof your work when you're wearing your glasses or contacts, and when you've cleaned your computer screen. And I can't emphasize enough the importance of doing a proper spell-check and being very careful about clicking "ignore." Your spell-check can't catch everything but it will do one hell of a good job if you use it properly. I have had many manuscripts delivered to my desk that clearly never saw the F7 key.

Chapter 7 — Common Spelling and Grammar Mistakes

"I want to suggest that to write to your best abilities, it behooves you to construct your own toolbox and then build up enough muscle so you can carry it with you."[13]

Stephen King

I could devote an entire book to this subject but instead I'll just highlight the errors that I see most often in the books that I edit.

The Dreaded Apostrophe

First, and the most notorious, is the misuse of apostrophes. In her book *Eats, Shoots & Leaves*, Lynne Truss extols the Apostrophe Protection Society. You may laugh but the apostrophe, correctly used, is becoming an endangered species. Many people don't know if they should use the term grapes or grape's. A grape is a noun and the only time to use grape's is in the possessive. For example, "The grape's smooth texture appealed to me" is a perfectly good sentence, but "Grape's for

---

[13]   King, Stephen, *On Writing: A Memoir of the Craft,* paperback edition, page 106, 2001.

sale" is absolutely incorrect, and you should demand that the owner give them to you for free if you see a sign like that.

This is also true for the word DVDs, which is frequently misspelled as DVD's. Wrong! Same with CD; the plural is CDs, not CD's.

Proper names can be a bit complicated. Let's say that the Macdonalds are taking a vacation. That means that all of the people in my family are going away together: individually, I'm known as Sigrid Macdonald but as a group, my family becomes the Macdonalds. However, if you want to visit me at my house, you will say that you are going over to the Macdonald's. Why? Because the apostrophe there stands in for the missing word house.

Other uses of the apostrophe are for forming the plural of letters (e.g., A's) and numbers (7's). "His parents were extremely disapproving if he received anything but straight A's." And, "No matter how many times he threw the dice, he always ended up with 2's."

You're and Your

Apostrophes are also used in contractions. Take the words your versus you're. The first word, your, is a possessive pronoun, and we use it to indicate that a person, place, or thing belongs to or is related to you. For example, your book, your mother, your royalties! The second word, you're, is an abbreviated form of the words "you are." The apostrophe is standing in for the letter "a."

There, They're and Their

Likewise with another common group of words: there, they're and their. *There* is an adverb. (And also used as a noun, "You take it from there," or as a pronoun, "Hi there.") You may say, "You live in Switzerland? Amazing! I've always wanted to go there." You would never say, "I've always wanted to go they're," because they're is the abbreviated version of "they are." To use it in a sentence, one would say, "Just because you're paranoid, doesn't mean that they're not out to get you."

Their is much like the word your; it denotes possession and refers to an object or person that is related to your subject. "Their house is magnificent."

It's and Its

It's and its sometimes create stumbling blocks also. The former is a contraction for the words "it is." The latter is a pronoun. Some people cringe when these simple words are misused. "To those who care about punctuation, a sentence such as 'Thank God its Friday' (without the apostrophe) rouses feelings not only of despair but of violence,"[14] Lynne Truss remarked in good humor, although one suspects that she was dead serious.

Don't Mix Present and Past Tense or Confuse First and Third Persons

Usually, books and articles are written in the past tense, and more often than not in the third person. For example, "Mrs. Hoffman was a terrible snob." But sometimes an article or book is written in the first person or in the present tense. "I cry during sad movies."

Both forms are correct, but you want to use the same tense and the same person throughout your manuscript or paper. If you're writing from the perspective of Mrs. Hoffman, an attorney, for the first twelve chapters, you don't want to suddenly start saying, "*I* was insufferable during my law school years" when you meant to say, "She was insufferable..."

And don't mix the past and the present tense. If the book starts out in the present tense ("David is playing his guitar."), make sure that you haven't inadvertently moved to past tense later on, in the paragraph or the chapter ("David drove like a maniac.").

---

[14]   Truss, Lynne, *Eats, Shoots & Leaves: The Zero Tolerance Approach to Punctuation, the Illustrated Edition,* page 49, 2003.

One Word or Two?

Sometimes, it's hard to know when to use everyday and every day, any more or anymore, mind set or mind-set, back yard or backyard. I'll tell you right off the bat that backyard and mind-set are always one word. Everyday is one word when it's used as an adjective and two words when the word day constitutes a noun. Any more is pretty much synonymous with additional, but anymore is equivalent to the word again.

"Every day I asked my teacher if there were any more assignments before midterms. I didn't tell him that I didn't feel like doing the everyday homework anymore because my mind-set was such that I would have preferred to soak up the rays in the backyard."

What about lifespan? Not sure if that's one word or two? Look it up. Bookmark Merriam-Webster dictionary online or www.dictionary.com. When in doubt, check it out.

Who's on First?

There's an old Abbott and Costello joke where Lou Costello asks Bud Abbott who is on first base and Abbott replies, "*Who's* on first," using Who as a first name. Costello responds with, "I'm asking *you* who's on first," and on and on it goes. This routine is so clever and grammatically pertinent that I'm including a partial transcript from Baseball Almanac.com,[15] and a link to the original video on You Tube, which shouldn't be missed.[16]

The boys are talking about a fictional baseball team called the St. Louis Wolves and Bud Abbott starts out by telling his pal that players nowadays have "very peculiar" names.

Costello: You mean funny names?

Abbott: Strange names, pet names...like Dizzy Dean...

Costello: His brother Daffy.

Abbott: Daffy Dean...

Costello: And their French cousin.

Abbott: French?

Costello: Goofè.

Abbott: Goofè Dean. Well, let's see, we have on the bags. Who's on first, What's on second, I Don't Know is on third...

---

[15]   Baseball Almanac.com, [http://www.baseball-almanac.com/humor4.shtml], website accessed January 10, 2010.
[16]   Abbott, Bud and Costello, Lou, "Who's on First?", You Tube.com, [http://www.youtube.com/watch?v=sShMA85pv8M], website accessed January 10, 2010.

Costello: That's what I want to find out.

Abbott: I say, Who's on first, What's on second, I Don't Know's on third.

Costello: Are you the manager?

Abbott: Yes.

Costello: You gonna be the coach too?

Abbott: Yes.

Costello: And you don't know the fellows' names?

Abbott: Well, I should.

Costello: Well then, who's on first?

Abbott: Yes.

Costello: I mean the fellow's name.

Abbott: Who.

Costello: The guy on first.

Abbott: Who.

PAUSE

Too funny! So when do we use who's and whose? Again, who's is a contraction that means "who is," whereas whose is a possessive pronoun.

Can I put all of those tricky little words together in a short paragraph? Let's see.

"You're never going to excel if you keep worrying about who's doing what in the blogosphere, and what they're writing about out there in cyberspace, if you're focusing on your own perceived defects and comparing your imagined deficiencies to their perfect copy. It's counterproductive to concern yourself with its importance and relevance to your work. Whose business is it anyway to police other blogs? Best to concentrate on your own."

What about apostrophes in proper names? Sometimes they look wrong, especially when the person's name ends in "s." Some people prefer to drop the "s" and just use an apostrophe with proper names that end with "s." An example of that would be, "John's grades were good but Silas' marks left much to be desired."

The Chicago Manual of Style provides clear recommendations for the use of punctuation and grammar. They advise using that extra "s" even if it looks strange.[17] So I would rewrite the above sentence to read, "John's grades were good but Silas's marks left much to be desired." Yet *Chicago* advocates removing the additional "s" if the original "s" is not pronounced. For example, "Albert Camus' literary career was impressive."

And there is an exception when we use the phrase "for someone's sake." "For Jesus' sake" and "for goodness' sake" are correct. But if we want to refer to the disciples, *Chicago* would write "Jesus's disciples."[18]

Not everyone agrees and our esteemed British grammarian, Lynne Truss, recommends always omitting a possessive apostrophe after the name Jesus.[19] She would suggest the following: "Many Christians were offended by the book *The Da Vinci Code*, which talked about Jesus' heirs."

What if you hate the look of two "s's" in a row? Do you have to use them? No, definitely not. This is a matter of individual choice; the important rule to remember is *consistency*. That will factor into all of your punctuation; it doesn't matter if you use one "s" or two when you're using the apostrophe in the possessive. Just make sure that you use the same format throughout your book or article, and you'll be fine.

---

[17]   *The Chicago Manual of Style*, 7.22, page 283, 2003.
[18]   Ibid.
[19]   Truss, Lynne, *Eats, Shoots & Leaves, Illustrated Version,* page 59, 2003.

Run-on Sentences

How many times do you encounter two ideas that are so closely related that you swear that they should be in the same sentence? "I'm running out the door, see you later" is a good example. Although it seems that those two thoughts belong together, they don't. Whenever you're unsure about whether a sentence is a run-on, see if the first part will stand up in a sentence on its own. If so, it's a complete clause and before adding the second clause, you want to separate the two with a conjunction, such as *and, but,* or *or,* a dash, colon or semicolon.

Just to be clear, a clause is a phrase that contains a subject and a predicate. "Jack won the Nobel Prize." In this sentence, Jack is the subject, won is the verb, *the* is the article and Nobel Prize is the direct object.

"Dominique sent her best friend a yearly subscription to *Psychology Today*." The magazine, *Psychology Today,* is the direct object because Dominique sent it. Her best friend is the indirect object because she received the subscription.

You don't have to memorize or even think about clauses at all. As humor columnist Dave Barry would say, clauses aren't thinking about you, so don't worry about them. All you have to know is that if a short phrase can form a complete sentence on its own, like "Jack won the prize," then before you add something else, such as, "He's really brilliant," you need to insert a period or the word *and, or* or *but.*

There are always exceptions to the rules. Sometimes you may want to run sentences together because it looks best, sounds great and is exactly what you want to say. That's fine. You can break the rules of grammar as long as you know what they are. Joyce Carol Oates, one of the most prolific, and in my opinion, fantastic novelists of the 20th century and a professor of English Literature at Princeton, is famous for writing books with endlessly long run-on sentences. Occasionally, she'll write an entire page without using a period! Usually, she's trying to simulate a breathless quality in her writing or to do a type of free association. She can get away with it. So can you if you do it deliberately, fully understanding what a run-on sentence is.

Know that a complete clause should be followed by a conjunction, but go ahead and skip them when they look wrong to you. This is often essential in prose, or if you're trying to capture a certain dialogue or a southern drawl.

No Ifs, Ands or Buts

When I was growing up, I was taught never to start a sentence with the word *and* or *but.* But that rule has gone by the board along with rotary phones. *The Chicago Manual of Style* says that it's perfectly acceptable to do so[20] and even preferable if you can shorten your sentence, rather than artificially dragging it out by fearing the use of a conjunction to open your sentence.

POP QUIZ ONE— this is a multiple choice test. Choose the answer that's correct. Print this out and see how well you do. If you score four right out of five, you're doing great. If not, come back and review this section later on. The answers are in the appendix at the back of the book.

Don't forget to make a note of the ones that you get wrong so you know where your weak areas lie. More than one option may be correct.

1. (a) I went looking at automobiles but didn't have the money to buy the Saabs.

(b) I went looking at automobile's but didn't have the money to buy the Saabs.

(c) I went looking at automobiles but didn't have the money to buy the Saab's.

2. (a) I love going to the ocean. The saltwater is so refreshing.

(b) I love going to the ocean, the saltwater is so refreshing.

---

[20] *The Chicago Manual of Style,* 5.191, page 193, 2003.

(c) I love going to the ocean. And the saltwater is so refreshing.

3. (a) Judas' betrayal will never be forgotten.

   (b) Judas's betrayal will never be forgotten.

   (c) Judases betrayal will never be forgotten.

4. (a) You're in big trouble for not filling up the gas tank any more.

   (b) Your in big trouble for not filling up the gas tank any more.

   (c) You're in big trouble for not filling up the gas tank anymore.

5. (a) They're house isn't far from here. It's just around the corner.

   (b) There house isn't far from here. It's just around the corner.

   (c) Their house isn't far from here. Its just around the corner.

6. (a) We don't have anymore presidents like John Adams.

   (b) We don't have any more precedents like John Adams.

   (c) We don't have any more presidents like John Adams.

7. (a) He wished that he could play hockey every day.

(b) He wished that he could play hockey everyday.

(c) He witched that he could play hockey every day.

8. (a) The autumn leaves are so beautiful, he refused to rake the backyard.

(b) The autumn leaves were so beautiful that he refused to rake the backyard.

(c) The autumn leaves are so beautiful that he refused to rake the back yard.

9. (a) She sings in the shower and then applied her favorite almond moisturizing cream.

(b) She sung in the shower and then applied her favorite almond moisturizing cream.

(c) She sang in the shower and then applied her favorite almond moisturizing cream.

10. (a) "Honey," Diana murmured. "Who's coming over tonight?"

(b) "Honey." Diana murmured. "Whose coming over tonight?"

(c) "Honey." Diana murmured. "Who's coming over tonight?"

Chapter 8 — Punctuation: Boring but Essential

Maybe it's time that you went out to the kitchen to make a strong pot of coffee. I know that some of this information on English composition skills can be dry, but it's a lot like math. There are rules in grammar and they are very rational, not arbitrary. If you can learn to view editing as a process that is concrete, specific and reproducible, you can relax about your ability to perform. You'll be able to do it; it's just a matter of relearning or remembering what you were taught in school. After you put in a few uncomfortable hours memorizing the basics, they will stick with you and become second nature. And you'll find yourself writing your first drafts without making the following mistakes.

What are the various forms of punctuation? We have the question mark, the comma, the serial comma, the colon, the semicolon, the ellipse, the dash and its siblings. There are em dashes, en dashes and hyphens, single and double quotation marks, periods and exclamation marks. What you want to know is when to best use these little suckers and which ones are most likely to give you grief.

The Question Mark

Obviously, you want to use a question mark at the end of any sentence that poses a question. It sounds like a no-brainer but often enough even the pros forget. In John Grisham's second blockbuster novel, *A Time to Kill*, he frequently omits question marks. On page 274, in the sentence, "Why don't you get it and get dressed,"[21] there is no question mark but there should be.

Likewise on page 282, one of his characters says, "What's today," he thought.[22] Now that's a particularly interesting sentence because to begin with, whenever we refer to somebody's thoughts, we should frame that part of the sentence in italics but Grisham didn't do that. And there should be a question mark after the word today, so the phrase should actually look like this: *What's today?* he thought.

Note that the word he is <u>not</u> capitalized because it is a continuation of the same sentence. The man is having a thought. That is very much like saying something out loud except that we will not add any quotation marks, but rather place the thought in italics, add the question mark and lowercase the pronoun he. I will discuss this further in our section on dialogue.

Some writers aren't sure what constitutes a question, particularly when the phrase "I wonder" is involved. "I wonder if

---

[21]   Grisham, John, *A Time to Kill*, paperback edition, page 274, 2009.
[22]   Ibid, page 282.

she's coming" is <u>not</u> a question. It's a statement. A question is, "Is she coming?" That deserves a question mark. Any sentence that begins with "I wonder" generally does not warrant a question mark, and there's no need for you to wonder anymore about it.

The Comma

I'm not sure why something as small and inherently benign as a comma can intimidate a grown man. So many of us don't know when to use it and when to leave it at home. There are two basic schools of thought that I've seen and you can follow either one.

The first school states that if a sentence has more than one conjunction (remember that coordinating conjunctions are words like *and, or, but,* and *so*), then you should use at least one comma. Here's an example: "I called my husband <u>and</u> asked if he would pick up the theater tickets <u>but</u> he said that he had to work late." There are only two conjunctions in that sentence and I've underlined them both. According to The Standard Deviants, that means it's not critical to use a comma.[23] But if we add to the sentence and alter it as follows, we want to add in the pesky comma. "I called my husband <u>and</u> asked if he would pick up the theater tickets, <u>but</u> he said that he had to work late <u>and</u> he

---

[23]   *Standard Deviants Master English Grammar 2,* DVD release date, May 18, 2004.

wouldn't have time to do it." Ah ha! Now we have three conjunctions and Standard Deviants suggests placing your comma directly before the word *but* or before the last *and.*

Think of the comma as a forced pause in the conversation. The more information that you cram into one sentence, the more likely it is that you'll add clarity to your meaning by adding a comma.

However, the other school of thought, exemplified by *The Chicago Manual of Style,* recommends using a comma after every conjunction.[24] Personally, I find that really slows the sentence down, but it is standard procedure and is perfectly correct. Therefore, if we took the above practice sentence and rewrote it the way *Chicago* suggests, it would read like this: "I called my husband, and asked if he would pick up the theater tickets, but he said that he had to work late, and he wouldn't have time to do it." (Another popular style guide by the *Associated Press* may have different suggestions.)

The only occasions that *Chicago* permits dropping one of those commas is when two thoughts in a sentence are related. For example, "I was tired and hungry." Both tired and hungry describe my physical state, so it's not necessary to separate them with commas. Likewise with this sentence: "After the funeral, Anil laughed and wept, and finally slept." His laughter and his

---

[24]   *The Chicago Manual of Style,* 6.19, page 245, 2003.

tears were part of his grief state and did not need to be punctuated separately.

It doesn't matter which rule you choose as long as you follow it every time throughout your manuscript or essay. Don't add in commas randomly whenever you feel like it and don't rely on your intuition. Make a list of the punctuation style that you'll employ before you start to edit your own work.

Serial Commas

Now we can move on to serial commas. A serial comma is used when you have a list of items. Let's say that you go to the organic market and purchase blueberries, strawberries, and cantaloupe. Those three items are similar, thus, we want to add a comma after each one if we are serializing our punctuation.[25] That's what *Chicago* recommends but not everyone agrees. Many people may write the above list by saying that they "purchased blueberries, strawberries and cantaloupe." Other people (couch potatoes) could say that they "bought potato chips, vanilla ice cream and hot fudge sauce." You catch my drift.

Introductory Clauses

Before we leave commas, I'd like to talk about introductory clauses. Those are clauses that can't stand on their

---

[25] Ibid, 6.19, page 245.

own. "When it drops below 20° Fahrenheit, I need to plug my car in when I park it outside." If you were to take the first part of that sentence and delete the rest, you couldn't leave the phrase there by its lonesome because it's a sentence fragment. *Chicago* recommends separating that from the rest of the sentence by using a friendly comma[26] but other people consider it a matter of individual taste.

What is essential in the world of commas is to standardize them and use them to make the material more clear. Think of your reader. It can be tiresome to sift through long sentences with many adjectives or separate clauses.

Speaking of adjectives, you also want to separate those by commas. If you're talking about your son's shiny, silver nose ring, make sure to separate the words shiny and silver. Same with "It was a long, stifling summer day."[27]

Colons and Semicolons

If you thought that commas were complicated, they don't hold a candle to colons and semicolons. Many of us have no idea when to use either one of these and frequently avoid them for that reason. But there's no need to. Here's the skinny; if you have a complete clause that can stand on its own, but you want to add a

[26]   Ibid, 6.25, page 246.
[27]   Ibid, 6.39, page 250.

related thought, use a semicolon.[28] If you have a complete clause that's followed by an incomplete clause, use a colon.[29]

"The week of February 12th is devoted to celebrating the birthday of Charles Darwin; I'm going to hear a lecture on evolutionary biology." Evolutionary theory was Darwin's baby so it is perfectly legitimate to link those sentences together, but not mandatory. The use of the semicolon is almost always optional, so when in doubt, leave it out.

Or you could say, "The week of February 12th is devoted to celebrating the birthday of Charles Darwin: the father of evolutionary biology." Why did I use a colon here? Because the phrase that followed was an incomplete sentence. It could not stand on its own. An easy way to remember this is to think that the clause after a colon usually doesn't have a verb.

Another instance where you want to use a colon is when you're reciting a list. Let's go back to our fruits. Here's another way to talk about the organic market. "I was so excited when I saw how many mouthwatering fruits were in season at the store: blueberries, strawberries, kiwi and grapes." Why wouldn't you use a semicolon in that sentence? Because the words following market consist of an incomplete or dependent clause, meaning that they cannot form a full sentence by themselves.

---

[28]   Ibid, 6.57–6.62, page 256.
[29]   Ibid, 6.63–6.69, page 257.

The Ellipse

An ellipse indicates part of a sentence or a quotation that has been omitted. There are two different types of ellipses. The first one is a three dot ellipse, which is used when parts of a quotation, such as a word or phrase, are deliberately removed. The second one is a four dot ellipse, which is used when one or more sentences are omitted in a quote.[30] This is often good for poetry or prose.

If you're continuing a sentence after you have inserted an ellipse, don't capitalize the next word if it is a continuation of the same sentence. If the next word begins a new sentence, then go ahead and capitalize that. Example: "As Abraham Lincoln said, 'You can fool some of the people some of the time…but you can't fool all of the people all of the time.'"

The Dash

This one is easy. There are two basic types of dashes, and then there is the hyphen. The two dashes are the em dash and the en dash.

Most of the time you want the em dash. It indicates a break in your thinking, and differs from the colon or semicolon because usually you want to say something important or dramatic

---

[30] Ibid, 6.16, page 380.

after your dash. It can be followed by either a complete clause or a dependent clause, and in that respect it's simpler to remember than the colon versus the semicolon. The only thing that's tricky about the em dash is that most keyboards don't have them anymore, so what you need to do is to type in two hyphens like this -- or you can insert an em dash in Word by simply typing two dashes in a row *without* a space. Word will replace them with the em dash. Or use the shortcut key CTRL + Alt + hyphen on the number pad.[31]

Alternatively, you can bookmark the website address for the Wikipedia entry for the em and en dashes; that's what I do. I visit Wikipedia, I steal their em dash, and I copy and paste it into my document. Once it's already in my document, I can do a keyword search later on and replace my other dashes. However, it is perfectly okay to use the two hyphens together on your dashboard, which will give you a sentence that looks like this: "Just before the new season of *Mad Men*, my DVD player broke down -- I was so disturbed." Using the one from Wikipedia, the same sentence would read: "Just before the new season of *Mad Men*, my DVD player broke down — I was so disturbed." [http://en.wikipedia.org/wiki/Em_dash#Em_dash]

---

[31]   "How Do I Insert an En Dash or Em Dash in Microsoft Word?", Computer Hope.com, [http://www.computerhope.com/issues/ch001084.htm], website accessed December 28th, 2009.

You can either leave spaces before and after your em dash or you can close those spaces, which seems to be the current trend. If you close the space in the last sentence, it will look like this: "Just before the new season of *Mad Men*, my DVD player broke down—I was so disturbed." Seeing that sentence so many times in a row reminds me that I'd better check my player before Jon Hamm and his dazzling Madison Avenue cronies return to the screen.

Moving on to the en dash. What's the difference? This one is often used to separate numbers. It's shorter than the em dash but longer than a hyphen. What if I want to tell you that I went to high school from 1966 until 1970? I could rephrase that by lying about my age and saying that I went from 1986 to 1990. Or I could use the en dash, stating that I went to high school from 1966–1970. This can also be used for miles, pounds or any form of numbers when you want to indicate a range.

In Word, move your cursor between two words. Add a space, type two hyphens, another space and the next word. This should turn into an en dash.[32]

Hyphens are also used within words. Often we want to hyphenate a compound modifier such as the term "brand new" house. We can spell that the way it is in the last sentence or we can say, "brand-new" house. I prefer the latter but it's individual.

---

[32]   Ibid.

Likewise, you can use hyphens within numbers. For example, twenty-two, forty-four or eighty-seven can all be spelled with a hyphen. And sometimes we'll encounter them in proper names like Jean-Noel, or a married woman who has retained her maiden name but added her husband's name, like Susan Richards-Market.

Single and Double Quotation Marks

Ordinarily, you want to use a double quotation mark to quote people who are talking and use single quotation marks for a quote within a quote. Here's an example: "It's ridiculously cold outside for July," Julia said, shivering. In that instance, we're using ordinary double quotes. But what happens when I change it to this? "John said, 'It's ridiculously cold outside for July,' but I don't mind because I loathe the heat," Julia exclaimed. Here we have John's words separated by single quotation marks because Julia is quoting John.

What if we already knew that Julia was speaking and she ended her sentence right after quoting John? Then we wouldn't have to attribute the statement to her by adding "Julia exclaimed" and it would look like this: "John said, 'It's ridiculously cold outside for July.'" Note that I put the period inside the final quotation marks and I used a single quote followed immediately by a double quote. I know it looks wrong! But it's correct.

That's the way it's done most of the time except for some European countries, like the UK, where the rule is reversed. There, basic conversation and quotations are put in *single* quotes, and a quote within a quote is separated by a double quotation.

The Period

The period is the most common form of punctuation. If the comma is used to indicate a pause, then the period indicates a full stop. Think of it as a traffic light. A period is a red light and the comma is a yellow light. We slow down for commas but we don't slam on the brakes.

Although a period is used routinely and looks as though it would be the easiest thing in the world to employ properly every time, it's not because of the risk of writing a run-on sentence. Once again, to avoid a run-on, ask yourself if two phrases within a sentence can be separated and stand alone. If so, either add a period or use a conjunction.

And beware of writing unnecessarily long sentences. Instead of just stringing your sentence on with more commas, don't be afraid to break a complex sentence into two by inserting a period.

A period is sometimes preferred to using a colon or semicolon because occasionally they can look pretentious. You

can't go wrong with using a period unless your sentence is
missing a subject or a verb.

The Exclamation Mark

     An exclamation mark is meant to demonstrate emotion.
You can use it for something that is funny, sad or surprising, but
use it judiciously. Don't say, "I'm hungry! What's for dinner!"
If you're that hungry, you may want to change your adjective and
say that you are "famished." That way you can leave out the
exclamation mark. Of course, if you've been on the Atkins diet
for the last six months and you're finally allowing yourself a slice
of pizza, that's different.

     Avoid using more than one exclamation mark. Writing
that is filled with them, or exclamations followed by question
marks (e.g., "!?!"), tends to look juvenile. Use them sparingly.
They will have a much more dramatic effect that way.

POP QUIZ TWO— this is a multiple choice test. Choose the
answer that is grammatically correct. Print this out and see how
well you do. If you score ten right out of twelve, you're doing
great. If not, you may wish to review this section later on. The
answers are in the appendix at the back of the book. Don't forget
to circle the ones that you missed and continue to practice them.

1. (a) I'm tired of writing — I think I'll call my sister.

   (b) I'm tired of writing; I think I'll call my sister.

   (c) I'm tired of writing… I think I'll call my sister.

2. (a) When are we leaving.

   (b) When are we leaving?

   (c) When are we leaving!

3. (a) "I was so shocked by his behavior that I could barely speak." she stuttered.

   (b) "I was so shocked by his behavior. I could barely speak," She stuttered.

   (c) "I was so shocked by his behavior, I could barely speak," she stuttered.

 4. (a) This semester he's taking algebra II, spanish, and chemistry.

   (b) This semester he's taking Algebra II, Spanish and chemistry.

   (c) This semester he's taking Algebra II, Spanish, and Chemistry.

5. (a) "JC told me that he would be late tonight. He said, 'don't wait up for me."

(b) "JC told me he would be late tonight. He said, 'Don't wait up for me.'"

(c) "JC told me that he would be late tonight, he said, 'don't wait up for me.'"

6. (a) "A friend of mine died following a double lung transplant: how sad."

(b) "A friend of mine died following a double lung transplant, how sad."

(c) "A friend of mine died following a double lung transplant; how sad."

7. (a) I've never been snowmobiling - would love to try it.

(b) I've never been snowmobiling — would love to try it.

(c) I've never been snowmobiling – Would love to try it.

8. (a) The red maple is taller than the house now: we planted it when we moved in years ago.

(b) The red maple is taller then the house now. We planted it when we moved in years ago.

(c) The red maple is taller than the house now; we planted it when we moved in years ago.

9. (a) I watched the show Are You Smarter Than a Canadian 5th-Grader last night.

 (b) I watched the show, "Are You Smarter than a Canadian 5th-Grader" last night.

 (c) I watched the show "Are You Smarter than a Canadian 5th-Grader?" last night.

10. (a) The Kennedy's assassination is still a cold case file as far as many people are concerned.

 (b) The Kennedy assassination is still a cold case file, as far as many people are concerned.

 (c) The Kennedy' assassination is still a cold case file, as far as many people are concerned.

11. (a) She'll be skiing in Colorado from August 8–10.

 (b) She'll be skiing in Colorado from August 8—10.

 (c) She'll be skiing in Colorado from August 8th until the 10th.

12. (a) I can't believe that Christopher is almost twenty one.

 (b) I can't believe Christopher is almost 21.

 (c) I can't believe that Christopher is almost twenty-one.

Chapter 9 — Consistency

Some of the rules of grammar are optional. You can choose how to spell numbers and which terms to capitalize. The important thing is to make sure that you have a system and you adhere to it.

Let's start with numbers. *The Chicago Manual of Style* recommends spelling out all numbers from one to ninety-nine, and then starting to use digits when you reach 100.[33] Other sources suggest spelling out the numbers from one to nine, and moving on to digits from 10 on. You can also hyphenate your numbers if you wish but you don't have to. That means that you can say twenty two or twenty-two.

It doesn't matter which one you choose. The only important thing is consistency. I can't emphasize that enough. Make sure that if someone is "age 22" on page twelve of the book, then someone else is not "fifty-four" on page forty. Some exceptions to this are when you are using fractions or making jokes like, "I'm planning to have 2.2 children." In that case, it's fine to go ahead and put in the numbers as opposed to spelling out the word, which would look silly.

---

[33]   Ibid, 9.3, page 380.

Everyone agrees that a sentence should not begin with a number that has digits in it. For example, what if you want to talk about 5,000 people who attended a rally? You could say that the rally was attended by 5,000 people but that's a passive way to phrase the sentence. If you want to be more direct, say, "Five thousand people attended the rally." I don't like to end a sentence with a digit either; I prefer to spell that out if it's the last word in a sentence.

Capitalization

Consistency is also critical with capitalizations. The tendency nowadays is toward lowercasing words. Words that we used to capitalize like president, prime minister, state, nation, and heaven are often written in lowercase now. It's a matter of individual taste and style, but please ensure that if you are spelling heaven with a small "h" early on in your book, don't capitalize it later. An easy way to check for this is to do a keyword search for all the important words that you're not sure about, in your manuscript or term paper. Just go to your toolbar in your Microsoft Word document, and right after "file" is the option for "edit"; use your pull-down menu, click the word "find" and then go to the tab that says "replace." You can insert the word "Heaven" in the "find" search box, and opt to replace it with "heaven."

This is where your list becomes an invaluable helpmate. For every essay, article, blog entry, short story or proposal, take out that list and itemize your own grammatical rules before you begin. You will spell out the numbers right up until one hundred; you will always capitalize The Great Room in your house because you like the way the term looks that way, etc. By having this list in front of you, if you forget your own rule halfway through your project, you can double-check it easily.

Some words are not meant to be capitalized. Take the word mother. Although you may worship her, don't capitalize the term unless you're using it as a title, akin to a proper name. "My parents refuse to consider alternative medicine; my Mom thinks it's ridiculous." Is that sentence right or wrong? Wrong! You want to say, "My mom thinks it's ridiculous." However, when you're referring to your mother by name or talking about her to a friend or sibling, cap that. "Father and Mother are nearly ninety. It's hard to believe that they're still in their own home." Or, "That's such a beautiful offer, Mother. I'm touched by your generosity."

In general, you want to capitalize a proper name, such as the name of a town, or a body like The Parliament of Canada or the House of Representatives. I can say that I'm going to the library and write that in lowercase, but if I'm going to the Ottawa Public Library, I'm going to capitalize that. Likewise with political titles. "When I was young I greatly admired the office of the president but now I view it as an unenviable job." Insert the capital only when you're referring to the president by name.

And remember that the word Internet is always capitalized. You can spell e-mail with or without the hyphen, but spelling Internet with a small "i" is not an option.

Characteristics

If a woman is on a diet and weighs 220 pounds in the beginning of your novel, and then she loses twenty-five pounds and consequently becomes 182 pounds, that doesn't work. Or if you've described a character as a loner, but all of a sudden he becomes very talkative and loquacious, that's out of character unless he's snorting white powder or moving into a manic episode. Are your fictional creations acting in ways that don't make sense for them? Be aware by watching out for these potential contradictions throughout your story.

Formatting

Standardization is extremely important in formatting. If you start each chapter of your work with your title in capital letters, bolded, in Arial font, size 16, make sure that every chapter reads that way and you haven't mistakenly started one chapter with Times New Roman in size 18. If you've left three lines between your chapter heading and your first paragraph, do that for all chapters. If every chapter title is centered in the middle of the page except for Chapter 9, which is off to the left, correct that. These are some of the important things that you can check at the last minute. You don't have to worry about them while you're writing.

Repeating Yourself

Check for repetitious words. Every author has certain words that he or she uses repeatedly — favorite words. There's nothing wrong with this but sometimes we want to vary our vocabulary. Or we're not aware that we used the same word two or three times in a paragraph, or three or four times on a page. Use a thesaurus and a good online dictionary like Merriam-Webster or www.dictionary.com. Find synonyms for words that you're using too often.

And be on the lookout for concepts that you have already mentioned. If you are explaining how beautiful your lake is in the spring, and you find yourself talking about the lake in similar detail in another part of the book, slash that, or be certain to bring it up again to illustrate a different point. Make every paragraph crisp and original. And do your best not to start each paragraph with the same word. Sometimes we can alter a sentence by starting out with a verb instead of a noun if we find that we're always using the same noun.

We are talking about Alex. In rereading our material, we notice that every third or fourth paragraph begins with the word Alex. Alex is off to the store, Alex is frustrated because his router isn't working, Alex's girlfriend is driving him crazy. How can we avoid starting each paragraph with the word Alex? Easy. Here are some alternate ways of phrasing the sentences above: *Off to the grocery store, Alex quickly checks his voice mail before he leaves home. Frustrated because his router isn't working, Alex loses his temper when he talks to tech support. Tired of being driven crazy by his girlfriend, Alex decides not to see her tonight.*

Contradictory phrases

Certain words just don't make sense together. For example, you wouldn't want to call someone "slightly psychopathic" unless you were being facetious. Someone is either psychopathic or not. It's like being a little bit pregnant. You're pregnant or you're not. End of story.

Words That Dilute

In the last decade or so, I've been hearing more people use terms like "kind of" and "sort of" in conversation. This has also popped up in writing and it diminishes the point that a writer is trying to make.

Oliver tells his roommate that uploading his Thanksgiving pictures to Flickr is taking hours of time away from his studies, and is "kind of a pain." Really? I'd think that would be a major pain!

If those phrases are a part of your vocabulary, be aware of them in writing. Sometimes, they may be perfectly appropriate. Standing in line at the supermarket for five extra minutes was "kind of a hassle." It was a minor annoyance. But in general, these terms slow down your sentence and detract from its meaning.

More Pitfalls

After you master the basics, you want to move on to more complicated issues in punctuation. The mistakes that I see most often occur within dialogue.

He Said, She Said: How to Punctuate Properly within Dialogue

At least half the time when I'm editing manuscripts, I come across the following: *"I just have to get out of this small town," She exclaimed.* Why is that wrong? Because the phrase "she exclaimed" is still part of the same sentence as "I just have to get out of this small town." The spoken words were simply separated by a comma but then the sentence continued. Therefore, you want to lowercase the pronoun that follows.

The same thing happens when there is a question mark or an exclamation mark within a conversation. "I'm going to go crazy if I can't get back to the city!" she lamented. Even though we have an exclamation mark and it looks as though we should be ending the sentence there, we don't, despite what our grammar program tells us. It will inevitably highlight the lowercased pronoun in green, indicating that it's incorrect, but it's not. So don't change it.

Ditto for the question mark. "Will you help me move?" <u>she</u> pleaded. You only want to leave one character space after the final quotation mark and before the pronoun. The way to master this easily is to read, read, and read again, particularly fiction. The more conversations that you see in print, the more likely you will be to reproduce them properly yourself.

What about Parentheses?

Most people know when to use parentheses, except they sometimes become confused about where to put a period within it. If your sentence starts out normally but you add a parenthesis, you will probably be putting a period after the final parenthesis. Here's an example. "George was eager to escape from his Geometry class (Geometry was his least favorite subject)."

I can rephrase that by making it two separate sentences, in which case the period will go inside the parenthesis. "George was eager to escape from his Geometry class. (Geometry was his least favorite subject.)"

Chapter 10 — Word Usage:
Round up the Usual Suspects

There isn't enough time or space to delve into all the various words and grammatical issues that can be problematic. But most people tend to be thrown by several common ones.

Like and As If

Recently, my mother said to me, "I feel like a bowl of soup." I replied, "You don't look like a bowl of soup" and she grimaced. Ordinarily the family grammarian, my mother would have been better off saying, "I feel like *having* a bowl of soup" unless indeed she felt wet, warm and slushy.

If you like ice cream, if someone is running like a bear, if it feels like 120° in the shade, that's the appropriate way to write it. But if you say, "I feel like going home," that's not optimal grammar. It's better to say, "I want to go home." And instead of writing, "I felt like he didn't respect me," write, "I felt as though…" or "I felt as if he didn't respect me,"[34] because the first phraseology is slang, but the second and third are not.

However, if you want to use that line conversationally, that's fine because then we know that you're simulating authentic

---

[34]   Ibid, 5.173, page 189.

dialogue. That works out especially well if you're quoting a teenager, who will not be speaking in proper sentences.

This is unrelated to the word "like" that frequently pops up in slang, especially for those under the age of twenty five or thirty. "I went to the movie and it was, like, so sweet!" It's perfectly all right to use that sentence in dialogue, but the grammar police will be all over your case if you use it in any other context.

I Feel Versus I Think

These two terms are often used interchangeably when they mean completely different things. Feelings are just that — emotions. I can feel angry, sad, wistful or inspired. I can also feel cold, hungry and sleepy. I can't feel that I wasted my money going to see a stupid movie but I can think that.

Thoughts are ideas in our head. I think about current events. I think that the earthquake in Haiti was tragic. I think that I've been sitting at the computer too long.

Be conscious of these phrases. Usually, the term "I feel' is the one that's misused. We're not likely to say, "I think I'm angry" or "I think I'm cold," but if we do, it doesn't mean the same as if we used the word feel. "I think I'm angry" means that I'm trying to decide if I'm angry or not; whereas "I feel angry" is a declarative sentence. Likewise with "I think I'm cold." That sentence implies that I may or may not be cold; there is an uncertainty that doesn't exist with the simple statement, "I'm cold."

If I Were King

    Tom Petty was right but many of us stumble on this one. When do you say, "If I were" and when do you say, "If I was"? According to *Chicago*, "If I were" is a subjunctive tense; it postulates something that may or may not occur, and most of the time it's unlikely.[35] If you just bought a ticket for a $5 million lotto and you want to tell your husband what you would do with the money, you're probably not going to win; so you would say, "If I were that lucky son of a gun who wins the pot, I'd buy a small island in the Caribbean."

    But if you are holding a lotto ticket in your hand and you already heard on the radio that the winning number very closely matches your own, and you're not sure if you have the winning ticket, you're safe to say, "Oh my God! If I was the winner, I would go out of my mind!"

    However, not all sources agree with *Chicago*. The BBC World Service has a website devoted to learning English. They say that "If I was" is the colloquial version that is appropriate for

---

[35]   Ibid, 5.127, page 180.

conversation, but "If I were" (or you, he, she, or they were) is the more accepted version for print. [36]

Affect or Effect?

Affect is almost always used as a verb. "The hot weather affected him adversely; he felt faint." Effect is the end result.[37] Think of side effects of medications. "The effect of standardized testing on the state of New Jersey was phenomenal." Effect is often another word for outcome. Affect may also be used as a noun, in which case it is referring to an emotional state or mood; "people with bipolar illness have an altered affect."

Is Everything All Right?

All right is always spelled as two words. Avoid the one-word version, alright.[38]

Between or Among?

Between is used when we are talking about two people. Use among for larger groups, unless there is a relationship between groups, such as trade between European nations.[39]

---

[36]   "Learning English," BBC World Service.com, [http://www.bbc.co.uk/worldservice/learningenglish/grammar/learnit/learnitv6.shtml], website accessed September 9, 2009.
[37]   *The Chicago Manual of Style*, 5.202, page 198, 2003.
[38]   Ibid, 5.202, page 199.
[39]   Ibid, 5.202, page 203.

Got That?

The word got is acceptable in conversation but generally, you don't want to use it in writing unless you're referring to the past tense of the verb to get. If someone asks if you got a divorce, that's a proper question because you'll sound uptight if you say that you obtained or procured a divorce.[40]

But when you're saying, "I got caught…I got laid off…or I got herpes" (the gift that keeps on giving), you can substitute a form of the verb to be. "I *was* caught...I *was* laid off...I *was* given herpes (or I contracted herpes.)"

Other times, you want to use the verb to have. We'll forgive Rob Thomas, formerly of Matchbox Twenty, for making a boo-boo in the song Soul: "But don't you worry, you don't worry, 'cause you've got soul." Sorry, Rob. That should be you *have* soul.

And lastly there are times when you can substitute the word got for another verb:

I got a new book today. I bought a new book today.

I got a letter from my uncle. I received a letter from my uncle.

I got homesick. I felt homesick.

---

[40]   Ibid, 5.202, page 216.

Feeling Bad?

Nine times out of ten, you want to say that you are feeling bad, not badly.[41] The only time to use the term "feeling badly" is to indicate that someone literally has a bad touch. "The masseuse feels badly;" that means that the masseuse did not have a particularly great technique. Maybe he was too rough or his touch left something to be desired. However, "The masseuse felt bad" means that he felt guilty or perhaps was ill. This is not to be confused with doing or faring badly, which will always require the "ly."

Feeling Hopeful?

It is common to use the term hopefully both in conversation and in writing. "Hopefully, it will stop raining this week." But that's not the original meaning of the word, which means "in a hopeful manner" or "I am hopeful."[42] Nonetheless, the new usage has taken over and most people will accept it as correct, but if you want to be old-school, find a synonym for hopefully.

It Is I or It Is Me?

Both are technically right, according to *Chicago*, but they

---

[41]   Ibid, 5.158 and 5.202, pages 186 and 214.
[42]   Ibid, 5.202, page 218.

view the former, "It is I," as stuffy and consequently prefer the latter, "It is me."[43]

Loathe or Loath?

Loathe indicates something that you can't stand. "I absolutely loathe that man! He makes my skin crawl." Loath is used when someone is reluctant to do something.[44] "He was loath to hit the books again so soon after midterms."

May or Might?

May is used to indicate what is possible or factual. "I may have left my car keys on the kitchen table." Might refers to something that is hypothetical or uncertain.[45] "We might have a permanent moon station in the near future."

Lay, Lady, Lay

The beauty of the Bob Dylan song title is that it will help you to remember how *not* to conjugate the verb to lie. As Grammar Girl says, this is also true of "Lay Down, Sally" by Eric Clapton. If both of these titles had been written correctly, they would read respectively "Lie, Lady, Lie" and "Lie Down, Sally."

This frequently confuses us. Lay means to place or

---

[43]   Ibid, 5.202, page 220.
[44]   Ibid, 5.202, page 221.
[45]   Ibid, 5.202, page 221.

put something somewhere. It's a transitive verb that requires a direct object. "Lay down your cards." It is conjugated as lay, laid, laid (e.g., present tense — "I lay down my cards." Past tense — "I laid down my cards." Conditional perfect tense — "I would have laid down my cards.").

Lie is an intransitive verb, meaning to recline.[46] It's never followed by a direct object. "Lie down and rest." You wouldn't think of saying, "I'm going to lie down my cards." It's correct to say that you are going to lie down but don't say that you laid down. The conjugation is lie, lay, lain, and it's the last two that we mix up, usually by saying "I laid down." Nope. Try again. Present tense — "I lie down every day at 4 p.m." Past tense – "I lay down with him in the tent." Conditional perfect tense — "I would have lain longer but the mattress was as hard as a rock." The best way to remember when to use lain is that it's almost always preceded by some form of the verb to have.

All or None

The words none, someone and anyone are all singular. Back in middle school, I was taught to think of the word none as a substitute for "not one." If I do that, I'm unlikely to misspell it by mistaking it for a plural. For example, "None of the guys were hot looking" is something that a young girl may say to a

---

[46]   Ibid, 5.202, page 220.

friend and that would be fine in conversation. But in writing, use the proper form, which is, "None of the boys was hot looking." By substituting the words "not one," we see that not one of the boys was good-looking.

That's the rule that I follow based on what I learned years ago but *Chicago* states that if the noun is singular, feel free to use the singular form of the verb. When the noun is plural, use the plural form of the verb. E.g., "None of the building was painted" is preferred to "None of the buildings was painted."[47]

Same for someone or anyone. "Someone was looking for you," she said ominously. Or, "If anyone was paying attention, he would have noticed the smoke drifting from the neighbor's house."

Time to Get Off

Never use the word *of* following the word off.[48] "Get off of that car stat!" should be "Get off that car." What you say when you're talking often doesn't translate well to the written page. You can be much more casual when you're chatting; I've even caught noted orator President Obama making grammatical mistakes in town hall meetings (but only once!).

---

[47]   Ibid, 5.202, page 222.
[48]   Ibid, 5.202, page 223.

After you've become extremely conscious of proper spelling and grammar, you'll notice people making mistakes everywhere, including the Internet, tickertape on the local news and in the newspapers. And you'll feel smug knowing that you wouldn't have made that error.

For Whom the Bell Tolls

When do we use who and when do we use whom?[49] Usually, you're safe to use whom when it's the object of a verb or a preposition. As the former, your sentence would read like this: "I felt nothing but awe for the woman whom I met the other night." As the latter, your sentence would read, "'To whom do you wish to direct your question?' the operator inquired." (Except that in real life, you'll rarely if ever hear an operator say any such thing unless she's studying Shakespearean English or mimicking Lily Tomlin.)

Mignon Fogarty, aka Grammar Girl, author of *The Grammar Devotional*, suggests using this rule of thumb: if the word in question can be substituted by him or her, whom is the correct form.[50] "To whom do you wish to direct your question?" can be answered by substituting the words him or her. "I wish to

---

[49]   Ibid, 5.202, page 232.
[50]   "Who Versus Whom," Grammar Girl's Quick and Dirty Tips for Better Writing.com, [http://grammar.quickanddirtytips.com/who-versus-whom.aspx], Episode 44: March 9, 2007.

direct my question to him" means that you want to use the word whom. But if you can substitute he or she, use the word who. "Who is delivering the lecture tonight?" He or she is delivering the lecture, not him or her.

Aside from who and whom, there are problems distinguishing when to use who versus that. The rule of thumb that I employ is that I use *who* for people and *that* for inanimate objects. Thus, "He's tired of the girl that he's been seeing" should be rewritten as, "He's tired of the girl who he's been seeing." This mistake is almost always made when using the word *that* improperly rather than *who*. It would be unusual to see something like this: "She put down the paintbrush to gaze at the canvas, who was looking stunning." What relative pronoun do we want to use for canvas? Which or that?

Don't forget to use your commas differently with that or which. There's no need for a comma before the word *that*. "She searched the entire hotel room looking for the tour guide manual, that was making her trip planning so easy." That comma is misplaced and shouldn't be there. However, if I want to rephrase the sentence by using the word which, the comma belongs. "She searched the entire hotel room looking for the tour guide manual, which facilitated her trip planning."

The Awkward Nonsexist Plural

Many technical writers now agree that it's proper to mix a singular noun with a plural pronoun. For example, writing "Everyone is deluged with work and can't find time for themselves" enables us to avoid the terms himself or herself. Most people still find this unacceptable, starting with yours truly.

It's not just a matter of political correctness for me. Why mix the singular with the plural when there are other ways to get around it? For example, "A writer should be aware of their shortcomings" could be rephrased as "Writers should be aware of their shortcomings." Often we're more cognizant of the need for the singular and plural to match when we are working in another language like French and Spanish.

Also avoid using the slashed version of s/he because it looks bad, and find creative ways around continually repeating he or she.[51] When I become weary of pluralizing my nouns, I sometime use he for the singular and later switch to she, so as to rotate them.

Fewer or Less?

Generally, you want to use the word less with singular nouns and fewer with plural.[52] Less refers to amounts of things:

---

[51]   Ibid, 5.202, page 217.
[52]   Ibid, 5.202, page 221.

less food, less mud, less beer. Fewer is quantifiable. It refers to things that you can count, such as fewer members of the school board, fewer new houses in the neighborhood, fewer diesel cars.

Lose or Loose?

If you lose something, it's gone. You can lose love or money, and then you're without both of them. You can lose your wallet but you can never loose or loosen your wallet. As an adjective, loose often refers to clothes that are baggy. As a verb, to loosen means to relax or release. "I loosened the chain on the door." "He loosened his belt buckle after the scrumptious Christmas dinner."

Thankfully

The word thankfully is much like hopefully: a bit deceptive. Literally speaking, it means gratefully or with appreciation,[53] but we often use it when we mean to say, "Thank God" or "Thank goodness." That's not really right. Try to say luckily or fortunately instead.

---

[53]   Ibid, 5.202, page 230.

Till the End of Time

Many people think that the word till is incorrect, or some form of abbreviation or contraction. It's not.[54] It's proper grammar to say that "The convenience store is open till 11 p.m." Till is not a contraction for until so don't spell it as 'til because that's not a word.

Till is often confused with 'tis, which is an old English expression that is a contraction for "it is."

Foreword or Forward

One of the most embarrassing mistakes that a new writer can make is to submit an otherwise excellent manuscript to a publisher and spell the material before the introduction as "the forward." Nope! Forward is an adjective that means near or ahead. "The car is moving forward." It can also mean brash, bold or presumptuous. "That woman was awfully forward by giving me her business card at the Rotary club meeting." Or it can be used as a verb. "I'm going to forward (i.e., transmit) my electronic airfare ticket to my brother so that he will be able to meet my flight in Miami."

A foreword is a preface. It's something that appears in the beginning of a book and is frequently written by someone other than the author. A foreword often contains advance praise or an

---

[54]   Ibid, 5.202, page 230.

explanation of the material that will follow. An easy way to keep these two separate is to think that a <u>fore</u>word is written be<u>fore</u> the main material.

Reflexive Pronouns

A reflexive pronoun is a pronoun that refers back to a noun. These include the words myself, himself, herself, itself, ourselves, etc. It's considered proper to say, "After a long and crowded subway ride, I was happy to arrive at my destination and be by myself." Or, "He looked at himself in the mirror and was happy with his reflection."

If I write, "Joanne herself met us at the door" that's called an intensive pronoun and it is used as an appositive or modifier. This usage is losing popularity, although technically it is correct. However, unless there's a particular reason to draw attention to how surprising this may be — "*Queen Elizabeth* herself met us at the door!" — it's redundant. The sentence would be much cleaner by removing the word herself.

A common way to misuse reflexive pronouns is by saying, "Paul and myself will meet you at the restaurant." That's wrong. "Paul and I will meet you at the restaurant" is right.

POP QUIZ THREE — this is a multiple choice test. Choose the answer that is grammatically correct. Print this out and see how well you do. If you score eighteen out of twenty-one, you're becoming a real pro. If not, you may wish to review this section later on. The answers are in the appendix at the back of the book. Don't forget to circle the ones that you missed and continue to practice them.

As always, remember that more than one answer may be correct.

1. (a) The Tragically Hip are a great band who I love to see live.

   (b) The Tragically Hip are a great band that I love to see live.

   (c) The Tragically Hip are a great band whom I love to see live.

2. (a) Now that my son is off to college, I buy less groceries.

   (b) Now that my son is off to college, I buy fewer groceries.

   (c) Now that my son is of to college, I buy less groceries.

3. (a) Marina tried to decide which iPod was most affordable.

   (b) Marina tried to decide, which iPod was most affordable.

   (c) Marina tried to decide on the iPod that was most affordable.

4. (a) I hope that we'll have a mild winter.

(b) Hopefully, we'll have a mild winter.

(c) Thankfully, we had a mild winter.

5. (a) I lie down my purse.

(b) I laid down my purse.

(c) I lain down my purse.

6. (a) None of the flu vaccinations were in the office by the end of September.

(b) None of the flu vaccinations was in the office by the end of September.

(c) Some of the flu vaccinations were in the office by the end of September.

7. (a) If I was taller, I would have a better chance at job promotion.

(b) If I were taller, I would have a better chance at job promotion.

(c) If I were taller, that would improve my chances of job promotion.

8. (a) I may go to summer school.

(b) I might go to summer school.

(c) I may have gone to summer school.

9. (a) I feel bad that your grandma is so sick.

   (b) I feel badly that your Grandma is so sick.

   (c) I feel badly that your grandma is so sick.

10. (a) I really loathe that man — he has an adverse effect on me.

   (b) I really loath that man — he has an adverse affect on me.

   (c) I really loathe that man — he has an adverse affect on me.

11. (a) After the long drought, the Zimbabweans drank the Red Cross water thankfully.

   (b) Thankfully, after a long drought, the Red Cross provided the Zimbabweans with water.

   (c) After the long drought, the Zimbabweans drank the Red Cross water gratefully.

12. (a) "Get off of that motorcycle or you're going to lose your allowance," Johnny's father bellowed.

   (b) "Get off that motorcycle or you're going to loose your allowance," Johnny's father bellowed.

   (c) "Get off of that motorcycle or you're going to lose your allowance," Johnny's father bellowed.

13. (a) Is it I being critical or was that movie really all right?

(b) Is it me being critical or was that movie really alright?

(c) Am I too critical or was that movie really all right?

14. (a) I'm, like, so tired of this.

(b) I feel like I've just been plugged into a wall socket.

(c) I feel like a bear before my coffee in the morning.

15. (a) Every construction worker faces danger in his line of work.

(b) Each construction worker faces danger in their line of work.

(c) All construction workers face danger in their line of work.

16. (a) I got really sick after dinner.

(b) I was really sick after dinner.

(c) Dinner made me really sick.

17. (a) I felt that it was time to move on in my job.

(b) I thought that it was time to move on in my job.

(c) I thought, it was time to move on in, my job.

18. (a) Cathie and I enjoy going to the movies.

(b) Cathie and me enjoy going to the movies.

(c) Cathie and myself enjoy going to the movies.

19. (a) There are hard feelings between me and my cohorts.

(b) There are hard feelings among me and my cohorts.

(c) There are hard feelings between my cohorts and I.

20. (a) Who will be speaking at the lecture?

(b) Whom will be speaking at the lecture?

(c) With whom will you speak at the lecture?

21. (a) Everyone deserves a chance at happiness.

(b) Everyone should enjoy their happiness.

(c) Everyone should enjoy his happiness.

Chapter 11 — I Can Trust My Spell-check, Right?

Be cautious about your spell-check. It doesn't work for everything. It's not like a calculator. A calculator is 100 percent accurate if you hit the right buttons. A spell-check will miss all kinds of words that you didn't mean to use but are indeed spelled correctly.

British and Canadian Spelling

Are you writing your book, essay or business article in American, Canadian, British or Australian English? If you're using Canadian English, don't spell the word favour with a "u" sometimes and other times without. Don't use the words favour and colour, but then forget to add an extra "l" in participles like dialing or channeling because Canadians use two "l's" in those instances.

Americans are much less apt to make this mistake because they don't know Canadian or British English. Canadians and Brits are prone to mixing up their language by spelling some words in the American style (e.g., gray instead of grey) but most words in their own tongue. The best way to remedy this situation is to purchase a good Canadian or British dictionary, and look up any words that you're not sure of.

Use Caution When Approving Words

There may be times when you go into your document and spell-check it, and you mistakenly approve a certain word or term. You may push "ignore" or you may hit "accept" by accident; in either case, in future checks in the same document, your spell-check may view that word as correct. Be very careful when you okay individual words to be certain that they are spelled right and used properly.

With a Little Help from My Friends

It's often useful to ask a friend to run a random spell-check of your manuscript on his machine. That will pick up anything that you approved in error, which will stand out like a red flag on your friend's Word document.

Don't Discount the Spell-check despite Its Limitations

Even though the F7 function is not perfect, you definitely want to take advantage of it in everything that you write. That includes blogging. Write your blog entry in a Word document and use the spell-check there. Then copy and paste your material. The checker in Word works much better than that in Blogger or other blog programs. This also includes e-mails, particularly those that are business-related.

Think Twice before You Press Send In All Circumstances

We're all busy — time is of the essence and we're always multitasking. But anything that you write in haste can come back to haunt you. It may be that a particular word has been used out of context, or that you've made a statement that you can't back up, because it's an opinion rather than a fact. It's worth taking a deep breath and rereading your material before sending it out into cyberspace where it can be endlessly reproduced, reread and misunderstood.

Mirroring

When I was doing my Master's in Social Work, I was taught to mirror the client's words. If someone told me that he felt depressed, I was to repeat that by saying, "So, you feel depressed." It seemed stupid and patronizing at the time, but it was meant to make the client know that, as a counselor, I was listening.

This is a great tool to use in e-mail or any business correspondence related to your blog, novel or short story. If a stranger addresses a note to me by calling me Ms. Macdonald, I don't want to refer back to him as Jimmy unless I'm deliberately setting a more casual tone. But if someone starts out an e-mail by saying, "Hey, I'd love to link to your blog" (or buy a copy of your book), I'll sound uptight and maybe even unfriendly by responding with "Dear Mr. McCustomer, thank you kindly for your inquiry."

Mirroring is also important in the *tone* of our e-mails. If you've been writing back and forth to someone, or you know a person well, it's fine to continue your note without saying hello or providing an initial greeting. But this may sound rude or abrupt if you do it to someone new who writes you a long letter, and you reply with one line that doesn't even have his or her name on it.

The more that we interact with potential readers of our works, the more attention we want to give to the e-mails that we send in response.

Chapter 12 — How to Perfect What's Already Great

You've carefully reviewed your work and eliminated a multitude of errors. What a relief. The material now looks terrific, but how can you take something that already looks great and make it fabulous? What other skills can you develop to improve your writing and editing?

To begin with, good writers use adjectives and adverbs sparingly, and choose them wisely. They also select strong verbs so that they can omit adjectives. For example, if someone is running through the forest rapidly, instead of using the word rapidly, we can say that he "sprinted through the forest."

Oftentimes adjectives are essential, particularly when you're describing characters. Make them unique. If you're talking about a twentysomething woman, don't describe her as "slim and angular with blonde highlights." Tell us about the little zodiac tattoo that she has on her left ankle, which indicates her interest in astrology. Talk about the pink stripe that she painted into her dirty blonde hair. If she's the corporate type, describe her man-tailored, gray pinstriped suit and the exact type of pumps that she would wear on a summer day when other women were wearing sandals. Be specific and be different.

Adverbs are another story. Much of the time we can do without them; when you do use them, think twice and be careful not to use the same adverb or adjective repeatedly. A strong verb can often take its place. Instead of saying that the clerk spoke very slowly, tell us that he stuttered, drawled or paused. Or don't tell us. Better yet, demonstrate it in dialogue, thus enabling yourself to omit an adverb. And please don't use an adverb every time that someone talks by saying something like, "…the doctor said, quietly." Much better to say, "… the doctor whispered."

Be on the lookout for passive versus active sentences. A passive sentence leaves us confused as to who is performing the activity. "The ball was thrown and Gerald caught it" is a passive sentence because we don't know who threw the ball. An active sentence would say, "The opposing team captain threw the ball and Gerald caught it."

Chapter 13 — Now I'm Ready to Submit to Publishers!

Well, almost. One last step. If you've followed everything above, your manuscript or article should be in excellent shape. As I mentioned earlier, devise a list before you begin your line-by-line edit and write down everything that you plan to look for. If you've decided that you will always capitalize the word czar but you are never going to capitalize the word governor, except as a proper name, put that on your list.

Add exactly how you plan to deal with numbers, and which words and phrases tend to give you trouble in spelling and in grammar. Write down how many spaces you're going to leave after chapter headings and the first paragraph, and if you're going to center your headings or align them to the left. How many spaces will you leave after a period? Previously, the rule was two spaces after a period; however, nowadays the trend is toward leaving only one space. Still, it's a stylistic and individual decision.

If you're using Canadian or British English, and you have any doubts or are aware that you may have problems with particular words, spell them all out beforehand or make a note to yourself that you'll look them up in a Canadian or British dictionary.

Then, after you have gone over everything with a fine-tooth comb, find a trusted friend or two. You're looking for someone who loves to read and will not consider reviewing your manuscript to be a chore — in fact, he or she will be flattered that you asked. You want people who have good writing skills. They may be fellow writers, colleagues, a spouse or a neighbor. The main qualities to look for in readers are intelligence, literacy and sensitivity to your feelings as a writer, but not so sensitive that they will be unable to provide constructive criticism.

Ask them to read your material. If you only want your readers to identify errors, just ask for that. Present them with your editing list, mention areas that concern you, and take them out for a beer or lunch as a way of returning the favor. And if you want your readers to give you specific feedback about the content of your story, don't take their comments personally.

Remember that we're all drawn to different material. I may adore Philip Roth but you may think that he's crude. Your neighbor may find espionage exhilarating but you wouldn't read it if it were the only source of print remaining after a quasi nuclear holocaust. Knowing that certain books and magazines appeal to different folks lets you view feedback from your reader (or readers) impartially; it could be valuable or it could be off target. You can decide what to accept and what to reject. And definitely take that person who plowed through the whole manuscript and provided detailed notes out for dinner or buy her a fine bottle of wine.

If you're a blogger, you may think about finding a blog buddy. Bloggers are often in a hurry, especially if they post often. If you can swap copy with someone else, offering to review his material for typos, spelling and grammatical errors, and vice versa, it will be much easier for you to find his mistakes than your own.

By the time you have implemented most of the suggestions here and received feedback from your test readers, your work should be in excellent shape. If you've written a manuscript, it's time to think about a query letter, a book proposal and a publisher who is just right for you. But that's a topic for an entirely new book!

Chapter 14 — Can I Ever Be Grammatically Lazy?

Yes! Absolutely. Many grammarians would disagree but I think there are times when you don't need to spell properly or to rigidly adhere to the rules of grammar. It's all about context.

Recently, I wrote an article called "Why You Should Misspell Words on Facebook." Of course, I was being facetious because you shouldn't deliberately misspell words anywhere. But on Facebook, MySpace and Twitter, type, scribble and tweet away without any worries about verb conjugation, word usage, run-on sentences and whatnot — if you're using it for social purposes.

If you're promoting your business on any social networking site, this recommendation doesn't apply. But if you're just chatting with friends and acquaintances, then you may be handling seven to seventy messages a day. And that's not including your real-world e-mail box, text messages and work-related correspondence.

On the job, we want to write as well as possible. This includes websites and blogs designed to be read by strangers, and to attract a high volume of traffic. But it excludes personal blogs that serve as diaries or journals.

The Internet has blurred the line between work and play. Suddenly, we're supposed to be available 24/7 and our brains don't work that way. Most of us are on paper overload; we are glued to our desktop or laptop, addicted to our BlackBerry, and feel apoplectic when our cell phone dies and we don't have a recharger handy. So I say draw a line between your professional life and your down time.

Writing a comment to your high school friends on Facebook and puzzling over whether to use the word lay or lie? Sending a text and unsure if you should say affect or effect? Who cares? Use Pig Latin. Your friends will figure it out. Don't take the extra time to perfect your writing when you're off duty. It will detract from other aspects of your life, and make you neurotic or overly self-conscious about making errors. Everyone makes mistakes on e-mail, text and on social networking sites. That's not a problem. It's supposed to be fun, not homework.

In fact, if you're carefully rereading *every* comment that you post for fun on Facebook, MySpace and Twitter from your smart phone, you're ignoring your job or class assignments. You're not spending enough time on things that are really important, like paid work, family and friends, and recreation (yes, believe it or not, there is a whole separate world away from your phone and your computer. Discover it!).

Writing for fun and writing for a living are two completely different things. Know what's what, and when you need to put in the time and energy to make your writing shine.

Chapter 15 — Three Years Later

All writing involves revising, reorganizing and rewriting.
Unless you're developing a college essay or a business proposal
that has a deadline, you have to establish your own deadline.
Some people are good at this and others aren't. If you find that
you are still revising your short story or novel many years later,
it's time to ask yourself why. What's wrong? Several factors
could be involved:

I. Your Writing Doesn't Say What You Want It to Say.

   Despite all of your hard work, your article, manuscript or
book proposal still lacks something essential. You can't pinpoint
it and you've gone over every potential obstacle in minute detail.
You're stuck, not with writer's block, but with genuine confusion
about how to move your project forward. At this point, you may
wish to join a writers' group to receive diversified feedback.

   Writers' groups are everywhere. You can join easily
online or look for one in real life; often your public library, or a
local college or university may sponsor a writers' group. This
will give you the opportunity to share your work and perhaps
read aloud, or post certain chapters online in a protected fashion
with people who you know will never steal your work. You can
always copyright your material first if plagiarism is a concern.

Visit the US Library of Congress at www.loc.gov. At the moment, the cost for copyrighting is $45.

Another advantage of the writers' group, compared to giving your work to one or two trusted friends or colleagues, is that by definition, a group is a number of people. Consequently, you will hear five, ten or twenty different points of view. While you may not agree with everyone, and they may not concur with each other, someone is bound to detect the remaining flaws or reasons why you're still unhappy with your material.

II. Perfectionism Is Rearing Its Ugly Head.

Maybe there's nothing wrong with your work. Maybe you just expect too much from yourself. We all want to be great writers. We dream of being on *Oprah* and writing The Great American Novel. That's fine but there is a limit to the degree of perfectionism that any manuscript can withstand. Perfect is an ideal and ideals are like utopia — something that we can only strive for but will never attain. Make your writing as good as you possibly can, and then pat yourself on the back and move on. Your best effort will be good enough.

III. Too Busy?

Maybe you started your book a while ago and lost interest. You're almost there — on the last lap — but you just can't summon the enthusiasm to finish it. This is often related to procrastination. Putting the final touches on an article, essay or manuscript is much harder than completing the body.

The best cure that I've found for procrastination is to make a to-do list and circle the item that I want to do *least*. That's what I'm going to do first. Then it's out of the way. I also set a timetable for myself: a self-imposed deadline. And every day I knock one of those dreaded tasks off my list, first thing in the morning. That way I'm free to proceed with the rest of my day with nothing hanging over my head. And one by one, however slowly I'm moving, as long as I'm in motion, I'll reach my destination. So will you.

IV. You Can't Identify a Finished Product.

If you're a first-time writer, you may not have any idea if your book is good or bad, or finished or unfinished. This is another instance where input from a group can be invaluable. Open yourself up to receiving positive, constructive criticism. If you have stumbled onto a group that seems fiercely competitive or unkind, leave. There is no justification for ripping apart another person's precious work.

You will know when the feedback is healthy and when it's not, but given the plethora of online writers' groups, if you can't find a decent one in your hometown, you will invariably find one at the end of your keyboard. The Writers' Site.com is an excellent resource; it lists dozens of local and Internet writing groups, and breaks them down by genre.

Keep trying until you find a group that is a good fit and ask other seasoned writers if your work is finished. Remember that your mileage may vary — everyone is different, so if person A says that your manuscript still needs a lot of work, but persons B and C say that it looks complete to them, go with the majority opinion unless it conflicts with your own inner voice.

And if you haven't discovered her yet, I strongly encourage subscribing to Grammar Girl's show on iTunes or signing up for a free daily e-mail. Mignon Fogarty offers fantastic advice and covers a wide range of topics. The only downside is that you have to listen to the same sixty second commercial on a short podcast; I use this time to daydream or wonder which people I've managed to irritate on that particular day. Seriously, the short commercial break is a pain, but the overall content is well worth your time.

V. You're Afraid to Release Your Baby into the World.

This is common and understandable. Many writers prefer the creative process to marketing. You may enjoy staying up late and burning the cyber-oil, and would rather write than submit query letters and move into other phases of publication and marketing. Maybe you're attached to your characters and hate to see them go. You may be afraid that your book will be a commercial failure and no one will buy it. If this is preventing you from finishing your novel or nonfiction book, which is neatly printed out, marked up and collecting dust in the corner of your den, sit quietly and ask yourself why you're afraid to let go of your manuscript.

If you're crazy about your characters or subject matter, you can always write a sequel or a related book. If you fear publication and exhausting promotional efforts, you can research them beforehand. Talk to other writers on websites and forums to find out all that you need to know to self-publish, or to send your manuscript to an agent or publisher. If you dread marketing, hire a virtual assistant or a teenager in grade eleven or twelve. All parents know that the best technical minds are in the youngest generation. Often teens will work for $10 an hour, in order to promote your work on Twitter or Facebook.

Delegate and confer with experts in the field. You don't necessarily have to spend money to do that; there are many online forums, discussion groups and blogs that are free and offer terrific marketing advice. Some bloggers offer e-zines that are chock-full of information.

There are many variables that may be holding you back from completing your writing project. It's important to identify them so that you aren't spinning your wheels and working on the same material years down the line. Be honest with yourself. Ask for help. Rewrite and revise if necessary, but once you conclude that the work is ready to go, simply take a deep breath in and send that bambino out to the universe.

Appendix

<u>Pop Quiz One</u>

Chapter 7, page 62–64

1. A

2. A and C

3. A and B

4. C

5. They're all wrong.

6. C

7. A

8. B

9. C

10. A

Pop Quiz Two

Chapter 8, page 77–80

1. A and B
2. B
3. C is correct because we assume the missing word *that*.
4. C
5. B
6. A
7. B
8. C
9. C
10. B
11. A and C
12. They're all right.

Pop Quiz Three

Chapter 10, page 106–110

1. A is preferred but B is acceptable.

2. B

3. A and C

4. A

5. B

6. All three are correct. It's just a matter of individual style and preference.

7. B and C

8. All three are right; although C sounds illogical, it may be used in a tongue-in-cheek manner or by someone who can't recall if she went to summer school many years ago.

9. A

10. A

11. A and C

12. They're all wrong.

13. C is preferred but A is also technically correct, albeit stilted.

14. They're all right. B and C are best in writing, and A is acceptable when quoting dialogue or using slang.

15. A and C

16. They're all correct but A is idiomatic; B and C are preferred.

17. B, although you can use A in dialogue.

18. A
19. B
20. A and C
21. A and C

References

Abbott, Bud and Costello, Lou. "Who's on First?" You Tube.com, [http://www.youtube.com/watch?v=sShMA85pv8M], website accessed August 10, 2009.

Allen, Moira. "Becoming Your Own Editor." Writing-World.com, [http://www.writing-world.com/basics/editor.shtml], website accessed January 24, 2010.

Bernstein, Theodore M. *The Careful Writer: A Modern Guide to English Usage.* Free Press: 1995.

Baseball Almanac.com. "Who's on First? by Abbott and Costello." [http://www.baseball-almanac.com/humor4.shtml], website accessed August 10, 2009.

BBC World Service. "Learning English." [http://www.bbc.co.uk/worldservice/learningenglish/grammar/learnit/learnitv6.shtml], website accessed September 9, 2009.

Cerebellum Corporation. *The Standard Deviants Present English Composition*, 1997, on VHS.

_____: *The Standard Deviants: Learn Writing Basics,* DVD release date, June 18, 2002.

_____. *The Standard Deviants: Master English Grammar 2,* DVD release date, May 18, 2004.

The Chicago Manual of Style: The Essential Guide for Writers, Editors, and Publishers. 15th Edition. The University of Chicago Press: Chicago, 2003.

ComputerHope.com. "How Do I Insert an En Dash or Em Dash in Microsoft Word?", [http://www.computerhope.com/issues/ch001084.htm], website accessed December 28th, 2009.

Fogarty, Mignon. *The Grammar Devotional: Daily Tips for Successful Writing from Grammar Girl.* Holt Paperbacks: 2009.

Grisham, John. *A Time to Kill* (paperback). Dell: 2009.

Helium.com. "How to Be Your Own Editor: 15 Articles." [http://www.helium.com/knowledge/15719-how-to-be-your-own-editor], website accessed August 10, 2009.

King, Stephen. *On Writing: A Memoir of the Craft* (paperback). Pocket Books: 2000.

MetroLyrics.com. "Matchbox 20: Soul Lyrics," [http://www.metrolyrics.com/soul-lyrics-matchbox-20.html], website accessed December 24, 2009.

QuickandDirtyTips.com. "Grammar Girl: Quick and Dirty Tips for Better Writing," [http://grammar.quickanddirtytips.com/], website accessed December 19th, 2009.

Strunk, William Jr. and White, E.B. *The Elements of Style.* Longman: 1999.

Toastmasters International. "Communication and Leadership Program, a Toastmasters International Program." Mission Viejo, CA: 1999.

Truss, Lynne. *Eats, Shoots & Leaves*: *The Zero Tolerance*

Approach to Punctuation (Illustrated Edition). Gotham Books: 2003.

WritersDigest.com. "Tip of the Day," [http://www.writersdigest.com/TipOfTheDay/], website accessed December 5, 2009.

Index

ABOUT THE AUTHOR

Sigrid Macdonald is a book coach, an editor and a freelance writer. Originally from New Jersey, Sigrid currently resides in Ottawa, Ontario. She has written two books, *Getting Hip* and *D'Amour Road*.

A member of Mothers Against Drunk Driving, The Association in Defense of the Wrongly Convicted, Ottawa Independent Writers, and the Editors' Association of Canada, Sigrid loves concerts, live comedy and watching Spanish movies, particularly those by Pedro Almodóvar. Visit her or drop her a line at http://sigridmacdonald.blogspot.com/.